A JOURNEY OF RICHES

Discover Your Purpose

A Journey of Riches – Discover Your Purpose

13 Inspirational stories for living a meaningful life

Published by Motion Media International
Editors: Daniel Decillis, Eric Wyman, Yasmin Phillip, Olivia Jayden, and Katie Beck.
Cover Design: Motion Media International
Typesetting & Assembly: Motion Media International

Printing: Amazon and Ingram Sparks
Creator: John Spender - Primary Author
Title: *A Journey of Riches – Discover Your Purpose*
ISBN Digital: 978-1-925919-64-6
ISBN Print: 978-1-925919-65-3
Subjects: Motivation, Inspiration, Memoir

Acknowledgments

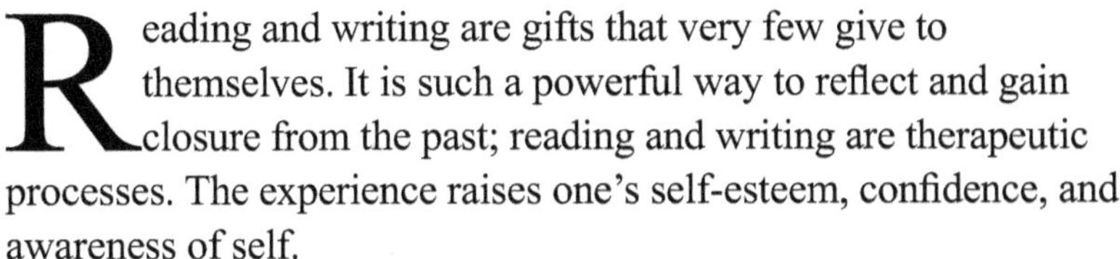

Reading and writing are gifts that very few give to themselves. It is such a powerful way to reflect and gain closure from the past; reading and writing are therapeutic processes. The experience raises one's self-esteem, confidence, and awareness of self.

I learned this when I collated the first book in the *A Journey of Riches* series, which now includes thirty-two books with over 300 co-authors from over forty countries. Writing about your personal experiences is difficult, and I honor and respect every author who has collaborated in the series.

For many authors, English is their second language, a significant achievement. In creating this anthology of short stories, I have been touched by the generosity, gratitude, and shared energy this experience has given everyone.

The inspiration for *A Journey of Riches, Live Your Passion* was born from my desire to share insights about living a meaningful and fulfilling life. Each chapter is written by a different author sharing their wisdom on finding their passion for creating a better life aligned with their purpose.

I want to thank all the authors for entrusting me with their unique memories, encounters, and wisdom. Thank you for sharing and opening the door to your soul so others may learn from your experience. I trust the readers will gain confidence from your successes and wisdom from your failures.

I also want to thank my family. I know you are proud of me, seeing how far I have come from that ten-year-old boy learning to read and write at a basic level. So big shout out to my Mom, Robert, Dad, and Merril; my brother Adam and his daughter Krystal; my sister Hollie and her partner Brian; my nephew Charlie and niece, Heidi; thank you for your support. Also, kudos to my grandparents, Gran, and Pop, who are alive and well, and Ma and Pa, who now rest in peace. They accept me just as I am with all my travels and adventures worldwide.

Thanks to the team at Motion Media International; you have done an excellent job editing and collating this book. It was a pleasure working with you on this successful project, and I thank you for your patience in dealing with the changes and adjustments along the way.

Thank you, the reader, for having the courage to look at your life and how you can improve your future in a fast and rapidly changing world.

Again, thank you to my co-authors: Jane Forkert, Renee Andreasen, Nadia Elmagrabi, Jenny Bot, Yiuvany Aguilar, Sandra Elston, Amanda Ray, Emma Flowers, Annette Korolenko, Maria Jesus Campos, Nerida Winters, and Marie Chandler.

With gratitude,
John Spender

Praise For *A Journey of Riches* Book Series

"The *A Journey of Riches* book series is a great collection of inspiring short stories that will leave you wanting more!"
~ Alex Hoffmann, Network Marketing Guru.

"If you are looking for an inspiring read to get you through any change, this is it! This book comprises many gripping perspectives from a collection of successful international authors with a tone of wisdom to share."
~ Theera Phetmalaigul, Entrepreneur/Investor.

"*A Journey of Riches* is an empowering series that implements two simple words in overcoming life's struggles.

By diving into the meaning of the words 'problem' and 'challenge,' you will be motivated to believe in the triumph of perseverance. With many different authors from all around the world coming together to share various stories of life's trials, you will find yourself drenched in encouragement to push through even the darkest of battles. The stories are heartfelt personal shares of moving through and transforming challenges into rich life experiences.

The book will move, touch, and inspire your spirit to face and overcome life's adversities. It is a truly inspirational read. Thank you for being the kind, open soul you are, John!"
~ Casey Plouffe, Seven Figure Network Marketer.

"A must-read for anyone facing major changes or challenges in life right now. This book will give you the courage to overcome any struggle with confidence, grace, and ease."
~ Jo-Anne Irwin, Transformational Coach, and Best-Selling Author.

"I have enjoyed the *Journey of Riches* book series. Each person's story is written from the heart, and everyone's journey is different. However, we all have a story to tell, and John Spender does an amazing job of finding authors and combining their stories into uplifting books."
~ Liz Misner Palmer, Foreign Service Officer.

"A timely read as I'm facing a few challenges right now. I like the various insights from the different authors. This book will inspire you to move through any challenge or change you are experiencing."
~ David Ostrand, Business Owner.

"I've known John Spender for a while now, and I was blessed with an opportunity to be in book four in the series. I know that you will enjoy this new journey, like the rest of the books in the series. The collection of stories will assist you with making changes, dealing with challenges, and seeing that transformation is possible for your life."
~ Charlie O'Shea, Entrepreneur.

"*A Journey of Riches* series will draw you in and help you dig deep into your soul. These authors have unbelievable life stories of purpose inside of them. John Spender is dedicated to bringing peace, love, and adventure to the world of his readers! Dive into this series, and you will be transformed!"
~ Jeana Matichak, Author of *Finding Peace*.

"Awesome! Truly inspirational! It is amazing what the human spirit can achieve and overcome! Highly recommended!"
~ Fabrice Beliard, Australian Business Coach and Best-Selling Author.

"*A Journey of Riches* Series is a must-read. It is an empowering collection of inspirational and moving stories full of courage, strength, and heart. Bringing peace and awareness to those lucky enough to read to assist and inspire them on their life journey."
~ Gemma Castiglia, Avalon Healing, Best Selling Author.

"The *A Journey of Riches* book series is an inspirational collection of books that will empower you to take on any challenge or change in life."
~ Kay Newton, Midlife Stress Buster, and Best-Selling Author.

"*A Journey of Riches* book series is an inspiring collection of stories, sharing many different ideas and perspectives on how to overcome challenges, deal with change and make empowering choices in your life. Open the book anywhere and let your mood choose where you need to read. Buy one of the books today; you'll be glad that you did!"
~ Trish Rock, Modern Day Intuitive, Best-Selling Author, Speaker, Psychic & Holistic Coach.

"*A Journey of Riches* is another inspiring read. The authors are from all over the world, and each has a unique perspective to share that will have you thinking differently about your current circumstances in life. An insightful read!"
~ Alexandria Calamel, Success Coach and Best-Selling Author.

"The *A Journey of Riches* book series is a collection of real-life stories, which are truly inspiring and give you the confidence that no matter what you are dealing with in your life, there is a light at the end of the tunnel and a very bright one at that. Totally empowering!"
~ John Abbott, Freedom Entrepreneur.

"An amazing collection of true stories from individuals who have overcome great changes, and who have transformed their lives and used their experience to uplift, inspire and support others."
~ Carol Williams, Author, Speaker & Coach.

"You can empower yourself from the power within this book that can help awaken the sleeping giant within you. John has a purpose in life to bring inspiring people together to share their wisdom for the benefit of all who venture deep into this book

series. If you are looking for inspiration to be someone special, this book can be your guide."
~ Bill Bilwani, Renowned Melbourne Restaurateur.

"In the *A Journey of Riches* series, you will catch the impulse to step up, reconsider and settle for only the very best for yourself and those around you. Penned from the heart and with an unflinching drive to make a difference for the good of all, *A Journey of Riches* series is must-read."
~ Steve Coleman, author of *Decisions, Decisions! How to Make the Right One Every Time.*

"Do you want to be on top of your game? *A Journey of Riches* is a must-read with breakthrough insights that will help you do just that!"
~ Christopher Chen, Entrepreneur.

"In *A Journey of Riches*, you will find the insight, resources, and tools you need to transform your life. By reading the author's stories, you, too, can be inspired to achieve your greatest accomplishments and what is truly possible for you. Reading this book activates your true potential for transforming your life way beyond what you think is possible. Read it and learn how you, too, can have a magical life."
~ Elaine Mc Guinness, Best Selling Author of *Unleash Your Authentic Self!*

"If you are looking for an inspiring read, look no further than the *A Journey of Riches* book series. The books are an inspiring collection of short stories that will encourage you to embrace life even more. I highly recommend you read one of the books today!"
~ Kara Dono, Doula, Healer, and Best-Selling Author.

"If you are looking for an inspirational read, look no further than the *A Journey of Riches* book series. The books are an inspiring

and educational collection of short stories from the author's soul that will encourage you to embrace life even more. I've even given them to my clients, too, so that their journeys inspire them in life for wealth, health, and everything else in between. I recommend you make it a priority to read one of the books today!"
~ Goro Gupta, Chief Education Officer, Mortgage Terminator, Property Mentor.

"The *A Journey of Riches* book series is filled with real-life short stories of heartfelt tribulations turned into uplifting self-transformation by the power of the human spirit to overcome adversity. The journeys captured in these books will encourage you to embrace life in a whole new way. I highly recommend reading this inspiring anthology series."
~ Chris Drabenstott, Best Selling Author and Editor.

"There is so much motivational power in the *A Journey of Riches* series!! Each book is a compilation of inspiring, real-life stories by several different authors, which makes the journey feel more relatable and success more attainable. If you are looking for something to move you forward, you'll find it in one (or all) of these books."
~ Cary MacArthur, Personal Empowerment Coach.

"I've been fortunate to write with John Spender, and now, I call him a friend. *A Journey of Riches* book series features real stories that have inspired me and will inspire you. John has a passion for finding amazing people from all over the world, giving the series a global perspective on relevant subject matters."
~ Mike Campbell, Fat Guy Diary, LLC.

"The *A Journey of Riches* series is the reflection of beautiful souls who have discovered the fire within. Each story takes you inside the truth of what truly matters in life. While reading these stories, my heart space expanded to understand that our most significant

contribution in this lifetime is to give and receive love. May you also feel inspired as you read this book."
~ Katie Neubaum, Author of *Transformation Calling*.

"*A Journey of Riches* is an inspiring testament that love and gratitude are the secret ingredients to living a happy and fulfilling life. This series is sure to inspire and bless your life in a big way. Truly an inspirational read that is written and created by real people, sharing real-life stories about the power and courage of the human spirit."
~ Jen Valadez, Emotional Intuitive and Best-Selling Author.

TABLE OF CONTENTS

Chapter One

SONIA'S STORY | Car Payments and Clockwatching

By Jane Forkert...5

Chapter Two

Wishing on a Star

By Emma Flowers...19

Chapter Three

Discovering my Purpose

By Nadia Elmagrabi...29

Chapter Four

A Modern Woman's Tale of Finding Freedom, Liberation, and Purpose

By Renee Andreasen..43

Chapter Five

Life Purpose

By Marie Chandler...57

Chapter Six

Discovering Your Purpose: Where's The Manual?

By Sandra Elston...71

Chapter Seven

Leaving a Legacy, Finding my Purpose by Seeing the Bright Side of Life

By Jenny Bot...87

Chapter Eight

Heal Your Story to Find Your Life Purpose

By Maria Jesus Campos...101

Chapter Nine

I Found My Purpose, Hidden in My Greatest Life Challenge

By Nerida Winters...117

Chapter Ten

My Story, My Journey Through My Eyes

By Amanda Ray...129

Chapter Eleven

Living with Purpose

By Yiuvany Aguilar...141

Chapter Twelve

Be True to Yourself

By Annette Korolenko...155

Chapter Thirteen

The Maze Of Discovering Your Purpose

By John Spender...167

Author Biographies...183

Afterword...205

PREFACE

I collated this book and chose authors from around the world to share their experiences about what "Discover Your Purpose" meant to them. This book is the collective wisdom of the various authors' journeys shining light on ways that you, too, can find and live your purpose. The eclectic collection of chapters encompasses many different writing styles and perspectives that embrace the intelligence of our hearts and intuition.

Like all of us, each author has a unique story and insight to share with you. One or more authors might have lived through an experience like one in your life. Their words could be just what you need to read to help you through your challenges and motivate you to continue your chosen path.

Storytelling has been how humankind has communicated ideas and learning throughout our civilization. While we have become more sophisticated with technology and life in the modern world is now more convenient, there is still much discontent and dissatisfaction. Many people have also moved away from reading books and are missing valuable information that can help them move forward with a positive outlook. Moving toward the tasks or dreams that scare us breeds confidence in growing towards becoming better versions of ourselves.

I think it is essential to turn off the television, slow down, read, reflect, and take the time to appreciate everything you have in life. Start with an anthology book as they offer a cornucopia of viewpoints relating to a particular theme. Here, it's fear and how others have dealt with it. We feel stuck in life or have challenges in a particular area because we see the problem through the same lens that created it. With this compendium and all the books in the *A Journey of Riches* series, you have many writing styles and perspectives that will help you think and see your challenges differently, motivating you to elevate your circumstances.

Anthology books are also great because you can start from any chapter and gain valuable insight or a nugget of wisdom without the feeling that you have missed something from the earlier episodes.

I love reading many personal development books because learning and personal growth are vital. If you are not learning and growing, you're staying the same. Everything in the universe is growing, expanding, and changing. If we are not open to different ideas and ways to think and be, then even the most skilled and educated can become close-minded.

This book series aims to open you up to diverse ways of perceiving your reality. It encourages and gives you many avenues of thinking about the same subject. I wish for you to feel empowered to make a decision that will best suit you in moving forward with your life. As Albert Einstein said, **"We cannot solve problems with the same level of thinking that created them." So,** with Einstein's words in mind, let your mood pick a chapter, or read from the beginning to the end and be guided to find the answers you seek.

With gratitude,
John Spender

"The real joy in life comes from finding your true purpose and aligning it with what you do every single day."

~ Tony Robbins

CHAPTER ONE

SONIA'S STORY | Car Payments and Clockwatching

By Jane Forkert

I'll tell you a story about Sonia. She lives in Yuma, a tiny dusty little town with a very old prison that's now closed to inmates but open to the public. She works part-time at the local Mobil service station and as a cashier at Walmart. She's been dating Clyde for the last eight years and still waiting for him to propose. Yes, he has problems; there's the odd night that Clyde would lose at poker, come home, and throw a few things around the lounge. So what? She has friends who have it a lot worse. Some got beat up every weekend; all it took was a skinful and the wrong look. Sonia had her faults too. She sometimes smoked rollies and didn't like babies. She would never hurt a baby but would not go out of her way to pick one up or even look at one. For all Clyde's misdemeanors, he loved kids and wanted a whole tribe. Her mother kept telling her how lucky she was.

"Your man wants a family, and he's a store manager! And he takes you to the movies once a month!" Sonia knew she should have been content, happy, but there was this niggle that raised its hand most nights when she lay awake. Snores on one side and the train rumbling by on the other, the net curtains filtering the amber light, she lay, wondering. Was there an alternative path? Had she missed the signs? Her eyes closed, drifting back to her dolls, Penelope and Susan.

The hours and hours she spent shampooing, conditioning, cutting, and blow-drying their diminishing strands of synthetic hair. Susan sported the mental-institute-escapee look with her curls cropped close to her rotund plastic forehead. Penelope now wore her mother's old wigs. Then, Santa delivered Tina. It didn't matter that Tina could walk, with some help, and say, "Let's do the dusting"; her full head of luscious dark brown hair with grey highlights made her the perfect next candidate for the chair. All Sonia's Christmases had come at once!

Sonia, at age nine and a half, had the organizational precision of a general surgeon. Her scissors, plastic curlers, combs, brushes, and clips lay like soldiers on her mother's best doily. Inspecting her instruments filled her with the deepest satisfaction. Tina sat, legs splayed, dark lashes shading deep brown plastic eyeballs. Sonia reached for the broad brush, gifted in a set from Aunty Peg and Uncle Don last Christmas. It glided through her hair, the strands parting between the bristles, smooth and caressed as they flowed down. Sonia's whole being relaxed, and her breathing slowed.

Stroke after stroke. Then it was the comb's turn, white with a purple flower motif, also from the set. Detangling done, Sonia parted and clipped and re-parted and re-clipped. She was about to start the ultimate, most joyful of joys – the cutting – when her mother walked in. She jumped as the morning tea tray banged down on her toy tea trolley.

"Oh, there they are! I've been looking for those!" Next in line for her client, her instrument disappeared off the doily.
"Mum. I need those."
"Sonia, they're a bit dangerous, love, and very sharp."
"But I've used them before."

Her mother gave her one of those 'are you telling me you've done something without asking' looks. "Just eat your biscuits. And don't forget; we're going to Granny's later. Be careful." The scissors returned to their spot, accompanied by a warning glance.

"Ok." Sonia wriggled on the stool. Finally, her mother disappeared with last night's water glass.

"Now Tina, where were we? Oh yes. You said you wanted a fringe." She combed through the front strands, covering Tina's pretty face. She placed the comb back and reached for the coveted nail scissors. The silver handle was smooth on her fingers; her stomach did that same little flip as when her cousin legged her up on the borrowed bay pony.

"Hold still, Tina." The noise of the nail scissors slicing smoothly through the synthetic strands was music to her ears. She felt like she was sinking into a warm bath of fragrant bubbles, scrubbed with happiness, and then wrapped in a blanket of bliss. It overtook everything. Nothing else existed. After the cutting came the trimming, water spray, and curlers. The whole process had rhythm, and there was a way of doing it. It had a certain structure, from the laying out the instruments to the order in which they were used.

"Oh, Sonia! You haven't eaten a thing." Her mother's head poked around the door frame. "Oh well, I'll just pack it up, and you'll have to eat it in the car on the way to Granny's."

Sonia looked at her Donald Duck clock. She still found the whole telling-the-time thing baffling but could see that the small hand had moved from 10 to 11.

"I'm going to leave you here now, Tina, and take these curlers out when I get home. You need a long time to set." She did a final spray-over with the water bottle. Standing back to survey her creation, she felt a sense of belonging. She wasn't looking for her mother to come in and tell her how wonderful she'd been. She didn't need her father to tell her she would make the best hairdresser in the world one day. She knew it, deep inside, so deep that she was sure no one could ever take it away or stamp it out. It was just her.

"Right, come on, in the car." Her mother's voice raced down the hallway.

Sonia grabbed her doll, Netty, short for Janet, her Granny. Netty had hair made of yellow wool and, so far, had escaped with only a trim of her plaits. "Coming, Mum."

* * *

Clyde spluttered in his sleep. "Hey babe, can you get me a glass of water?"

The illuminated green numbers read 6.10 am. Sonia slipped into her sheepskin slippers, a present from her father, and headed into the kitchen. As she reached for the pantry door, she imagined it being door number two, her alternative life. What if it was that easy?

"Hurry up, love; my throat's killing me."

Sonia passed Clyde his large glass of water, resisting the temptation to saturate his receding hairline. Instead, she turned her thoughts to the day ahead.

"I think I might pop in and see Erin today."

"What do you want to do that for? Don't you have better things to do on your day off? I thought you hated her." Clyde sat up and grabbed one of her pillows to lean against.

"I don't hate her."
"You do. You said she thinks that she's a cut above her station."

"What?"
"You think she's up herself."
"Well, I think she's done very well for herself."
"Okay, change your tune then. She has done well for herself; she looks the same as when we were at school."

Sonia slunk out into the hall. She didn't have the energy to pop into Erin's salon that day. She phoned. Long overdue for a wash and cut, it was time to push the boat out. Clyde didn't need to know how much it cost.

The following Tuesday, her knotted stomach was postponed. Wishing the crack in the sidewalk would widen to swallow her up or at least catch the impending vomit. She was on the verge of running when hit by the smells, the scissors, and the banter between clients and magical dryer-wielding gods and goddesses. She floated through the door and inhaled it all.

"Hey Sonia, how's it going?" Erin smiled. Sonia took her all in; Prada heels, Gucci pants, and God knows who on top. That sounds familiar! Don't go there; that's not what we're here for. Be nice.

"Hey, Erin. You look amazing."
"Oh, you're very sweet. Come sit." She motioned to an empty leather chair, gleaming chrome, perfectly positioned footstool.
"Thank you."
"Now. What are we doing today?"
"Oh, are you doing my hair?"
"Yes. Nothing but the best for Walmart's top cashier."
"Oh, you heard?" Sonia couldn't make out whether Erin was taking the piss or not.
"Yes, well, saw it in the paper. Congratulations, you would've had some tough competition."
"Oh, I think it goes on consistency. I turn up for work every day and don't have much time off."
"Well, I'm sure you deserve it." She paused. "You know. I was gutted when you turned down my offer."
"You were?"
"Yes, I thought you and I would've made a great team."
"Really? I wasn't sure since that thing with Clyde and everything."
"Oh, that. We were never going to make it. The stars didn't align. Values didn't match. Call it what you will. He wasn't for me."
"But I thought he dumped you."
"Oh no. It was pretty much mutual. I suggested it, and he jumped at the idea. I think he already had someone else lined up." She winked into the mirror. "Now, this hair. I love the length, but how about some layers?"

* * *

Sonia looked up from her boiling pot of soup at the sound of the screen door slamming shut.

"Hi honey, I'm home." Clyde liked to imitate the latest thing on TV. It made her laugh.

"Hey, babe. I'm doing soup, hope that's okay. I'll also chuck a chicken schnitzel in the pan for you."

"Perfect." He kissed her on the side of the head and squeezed her. She swung her head around.

Clyde stepped back as her hair flicked across his face. "What the…. Oh… Yes. Your hair looks lovely. Amazing. Fantasimo!" He kissed his fingertips in true Soprano style.

"Why, thank you, kind sir."

"So? How was it?"
"How was what?" Sonia evaded the obvious.
"How was the salon experience? My shout, by the way."
"Seriously? That's really lovely of you." And surprising, she thought.
"Did you see Erin?"
"Yes, we had a lovely catch-up."
"And…?"
"And… nothing. It was a very nice arvo. Free coffee and biscuits. Latest mags. Scalp massage. Couldn't have been better."
"Cool." Clyde placed his hand on her hip. It had been a while, but he knew the exact spot. The spot that made her feel they fit.

After dinner, Clyde suggested an early night. He didn't have his third beer. Or his second, for that matter. Sonia wondered if it was the new 'do' or a pay rise. Whatever it was, she wanted it to keep going, vowing to style and blow-dry religiously. She didn't tell Clyde about her conversation with Erin. She wasn't sure if he would agree and wanted to keep it to herself. Their salon chat had fanned that fading ember inside her gut, rekindled with the dream of her childhood beauty parlor. She felt the orange glow of excitement swell. Somehow telling people would be like blowing out the candles on a birthday cake. It's funny how you make a wish after and never thought of this before, but now it seems like it should be the complete opposite. You'd think a candle would be lit after you make your wish to symbolize that fire of passion within.

The next morning, Clyde was out the door earlier than usual, leaving Sonia time to herself. She dug out a notebook, tore out the used pages, and scanned them.

Make affirmations every night.
Do a vision board and look at it every day.
Be kind to everyone.
Imagine that you are who you want to be.

Mm… It seems like fluffing around. Surely there's more to it than that. She glanced at her Cashier of the Week certificate; *that could do with a dust*, she thought.

The bin pedal flicked open the lid with a crash, and the paper strips glided in. Now, where do I start? Looking down at the new page with the torn margin, she wrote:
What I would love to be on this planet: A hairdresser whose clients walk out feeling like movie stars. They are the happiest they've ever been with a haircut that brings out who they are inside.

What to do next:
The end of the pen flicked over her lips. She stared out the window and sighed. Nothing. Re-reading her statement, she let her mind wander, imagining herself standing in her salon, greeting clients, and then waving them goodbye with huge smiles on their faces. She could feel the joy of it bubble up. She looked around the salon, Italian tiles, crystal light fittings, chrome, and red leather chairs—the smell of the styling lotion on the tip of her nose.

Wow! Just wow!

Her tea was half cold, but she didn't notice, back in the tiny kitchen, peeling paint and scorched tiles behind the stove. She looked at the clock; time to leave in 45 minutes; Walmart awaited. Then back home, change, and be at the service station by 6 pm. Clyde will have to fend for himself. He wouldn't mind, as vegetables could go by the wayside. She thought of Clyde. His love, his laughter. She saw their life together as it is right now, working hard, one step forward, two steps back. Forfeiting their holiday and pasting on smiles for the Walmart customers. Looking back down at the notebook, she saw again her salon, the Italian tiles, the crystal light fittings, the pure joy of serving the smiles walking out of the clear glass door. It hit her like a ton of bricks. Like a bolt from the blue.

She wrote.
Buy a hairdressing kit.
Her pen immediately sprung back to the start, and a line went through the 'B.' She paused. *What harm would it do to buy one? Clyde wouldn't need to know. I could keep it in the bottom of my work bag. Don't be stupid; why spend all that money when I'm not even a trained hairdresser*? The pointy scissors from the first aid kit worked fine when Sonia's friends begged for a quick trim.

* * *

"Thank you. Have a nice day." Sonia clanged the till shut, leaned forward, and screwed her head to see past the stand of cheap umbrellas.

"You have somewhere to be?" On checkout twelve, Selma twisted her enormous body on the squeaky stool.
"Umm… yeah… sort of." Sonia stuttered.
"That's about the three hundredth time you've looked at that dang clock." Selma ignored the customer standing in front of her. "If I didn't know any better, I'd say you have Keanu Reeves holed up in a motel round the corner. Either that or you know something we don't."

"I wish." Sonia laughed. "And no. Today is not the day I blow up Walmart."

Selma swiveled back around at a snail's speed. "Good morning, Sir. Oh nice, very nice." She picked up the bunch of flowers from the conveyor belt. "These will do just nicely. Doesn't your wife like lilies, though?"
The pinstripe man on the other side of the counter moved his shoulders and pulled at the top of his buttoned-up shirt. Clearing his throat, he whipped out three twenty-dollar bills, snatched the flowers, and strode out.

"Selma!" reprimanded Sonia. "You have to stop doing that."
"What? What am I doin'? Seein' the truth?"
"Saying the truth more like."
Selma laughed. A deep-down belly laugh ran right through her Mama and Great Nana.
Sonia smiled. She'd miss this. "Right, I'm off. See you after lunch."
"Bye now. Don't go spendin' too much of your hard-earned cash on them shearing tools."
Sonia gave a thumbs up. How the hell did she know these things?

Sally Beauty was only a few minutes up the road, thank goodness. Plenty of time to browse and dream. She hadn't realized how many types of scissors there were. How many combs should she get?
"Can I help you?" A tall girl that looked about twelve wavered beside her. Willowy and wistful, she stared out the window toward the saddlery shop over the road.
"Yes, actually. Which scissors are the best for all-purpose cutting?" Sonia raised her voice.
"Oh, these." Without looking, she plucked a packet from the stand.
"Are you sure?"
"Yeah, it's what everyone gets."
"Okay then. And…" Sonia paused. "Um… I think I'm okay now, thanks."
"Just yell out if you need anything else."

She ambled off toward the counter. Only then did Sonia notice that her attire differed from the other girls in the shop. Instead, she wore what looked like English riding boots and a tweed men's dress jacket. Each to their own, she thought.

Shit, she looked in her basket with the lonely scissors, glanced at her watch, and set off at a defiant pace down each aisle. Scanning the products on either side, every three or four steps, one would jump out at her. It would make itself known. She didn't hesitate, and boom – in the basket. It was like she was in another zone; nothing else mattered. *Wow, this feels like I'm a superhero on a mission to save all hair tragedies across Arizona... the world!*

At the counter, the horse girl scanned and packed her haul.
"Sorry, could you go a bit faster? I need to be back at work in less than five minutes."
"Okay."
"Just a bit faster."
"I'm going as fast as I can."
"Sorry." Sonia thought about a staff training they'd had a few weeks back and brought her attention to her breath. Just noticing, as the guy had said. Then took her attention to her body, mentally scanning from her feet up. Slowly. Noticing the different sensations.

"There you go, that'll be two hundred and thirty-eight dollars exactly." The girl pushed the digital terminal toward her.
"I have cash." Sonia heard the words come out of her mouth while reaching for her wallet. Her thoughts were jumping in the background, and the brakes were coming on. She fumbled with her purse. "Um, I'll just see if I have enough." *Crazy. What the hell am I doing? I never have that amount of cash in there.* She opened her wallet and pulled out five fifty-dollar notes and two twenties. "Here you go." Her voice raised an octave.

The girl's long slender hand wrapped around the notes and returned with the change.
Sonia dropped one dollar onto the counter.
"Thanks.... Thank you. Um... actually, I'm not sure I need all this..." She tailed off, thinking about the forthright feeling of being in the zone, striding down those aisles. *I am a superhero hairdresser.* She recovered the dollar bill and swooped up her

'Sally Beauty' carry bag. Bolting toward her work, she knew what she had to do.

At home that night, she lit the tall gold candles in the look-alike crystal holders. Dinner smelled amazing; she always put a different swing on Clyde's favorite. Watching the flame flicker and then stand tall reminded her of her earlier stumble. How easily her thoughts had put her off balance and how simple it was to say that one thing. It wasn't like she was lying to herself, either. It felt incredibly true for her. Hell, she may even get a cape. God knows she already had enough tights to choose from. The funniest thing, though, wasn't even the words or the image it conjured up; it was the feeling that ran through her body. Total bliss, joy, love. It brought tears to her eyes when she said it.

By the time Clyde had had his second helping of chocolate sauce pudding, Sonia had decided his coherency would be impaired enough by the imminent food coma.
"What! You spent the car payment on scissors!"
"Not just scissors, combs, brushes, clips, rollers… "
"Jesus Christ, Sonia!"
"It's okay. Really. When I leave Walmart, I'll get my holidays paid out. We never did do that trip away."
"Shit. What if the car gets repossessed? How will I look to the boys then?"
"Clyde. I have to do this. But… if you think…" Sonia's lip trembled. She could smell her mother's musky perfume and feel herself sinking away into being nothing. *I am a superhero hairdresser!* "Clyde. I love you. I also love myself. And I would love to be the best hairdresser this side of Joshua Tree that makes her clients the happiest they've been with a haircut. Ever. A haircut that brings out who they really are." She braced herself, but the eyes she stared into softened.

"I love you too." He reached over and squeezed her hand. "We better get you a new pair of gloves, don't want those precious assets to shrivel up in the dishwater anymore."
Sonia squeezed back.

* * *

Poised, smiling, aiming a large pair of black-handled shearing scissors at a taut red ribbon, Sonia read the printing on it – "I now declare Hairdressing Heroes Salon II open." The emerald Versace cape lifted in the wind, revealing more of the Ralph Lauren riding tights. The champagne flowed, and the accolades came thick and fast.
"Congratulations!" Erin's smile spread across her whole face. "You're glowing. This life suits you."
"Thank you. I love every bit of it, the clients, the freedom to live by my schedule, and the travel. I'll never forget you taking me on after all those years. And if it wasn't for your help when I got Covid, I may not even have Heroes I."
"That's what friends are for. Just glad you changed your mind; you were very easy to train." She grabbed Sonia's left hand. "And what is this?"
Sonia's turn to smile. A genuine, no facade big old grin.
"That's one huge rock."
"Oh, it's one of those ethically mined ones."
"Well, it's gorgeous." Erin glanced at Clyde hovering by the canapes. "I'll leave you to it." She moved off, winking at Clyde as he passed.

"Congratulations!" Clyde swooped her up. "You did well, love."
"Hey babe, thanks." She surveyed the salon. The Italian tiles, the crystal light fittings, the red leather chairs, and the chrome. "Who would've thought all this in only five years."
"Yep, you're a bloody hero, my own Wonder Woman." Clyde placed Sonia back on solid ground and leaned forward so she could kiss his cheek.
"Ooh, I'll take that. Actually, superhero hairdresser, who knows her heart and follows through on it, regardless."
"Regardless of what?"
"Oh, you know, this and that. Car payments and clockwatching."
"Well, superhero hairdresser, let's get you home."

Sonia looked around at the near-empty salon. *I am home.*

“The purpose of life is to discover your gift. The work of life is to develop it. The meaning of life is to give your gift away.”

~ David Viscott

CHAPTER TWO

Wishing on a Star

By Emma Flowers

Part One

When I think of the phrase "written in the stars," I like to imagine an invisible pen writing my hopes and dreams on thin sheets of gold, which act as the flares of a shooting star, and then, I would make a wish!

Maybe our purpose in life is written in the stars from the moment we're born, with perhaps a small percentage of people lucky enough to know what it is. Others are still searching and trying to discover one thing to validate their life. I believe timing plays a significant role; for example, if you have felt lost for a while, something out of the ordinary breaks forth and inspires you. Suddenly you have a plan, a vision, a dream, or at best, the drive to do something else. In my mind, the doors we open lead to different avenues in finding our purpose, and we may not realize it at the time. At least, that's what I think.

What is your purpose? Is it to follow in your family's footsteps, take over a business, travel the world and visit as many places as possible, have a fruitful career, or devote your entire life to a greater cause? It can be as ambitious as you want it to be; of course, not everyone desires to be famous or run for the presidency; I know I don't. Some people I've met are still trying to find the 'X' that marks the spot to discover their true purpose and meaning. Others, like my parents, are more content to lead simpler lives. An example would be my father, who gave up pursuing a singing career in the 1960s because he wasn't keen on touring and the sacrifice that came with it. But if he hadn't explored that avenue, he might still wonder, "What if…?" Nowadays, he is a contented family man, living a comfortable life of growing and cooking his garden produce. It takes all sorts to make the world go round; society needs an eclectic mix of 'left brain,' 'right brain,' curious beings which we are, who simultaneously, along the way, might be helping others find their path. Me? I'm a writer, a dreamer, and a visionary, but I hadn't always known my purpose.

As a child, my thoughts and feelings would run away, and I often impersonated different TV characters in front of my family. I just loved singing, dancing, and stories! I remember my first book from when I was a little girl; my mother gifted me the story of Thumbelina; that's when I fell in love with fairy tales and fantasy. I was born into a loving family, with me being the eldest daughter of three girls. Life was good, but not without its challenges.

My parents came from low economic backgrounds; after they married in their home country of Italy, they decided to immigrate to the UK for a better life. I guess you could say that was their purpose. Having younger sisters was fun; naturally, I was the director at playtime. I would devise a silly script, loosely speaking, and using an old tape recorder, we would act out a scene, which usually lasted less than a short film. Then, at Christmas, my sisters and I would put on a little show for my parents, coerced by me. But, for me, being creative was so much fun!

At school, my favorite subjects were English, history, and art. Occasionally, I would visit the public library with my best friend; we were only young girls then, with nothing better to do on a rainy day. It soon became apparent that this bibliophile's hangout would be my sanctuary from daily life, with many stories to escape in, and in those days, it was Google central. Unbeknownst to me, a pattern of creativity began forming in my head while I was growing up.

Part two

By the time I was a young adult, I had written a few songs, some poetry, and a couple of short stories, purely as a hobby while reading the occasional book. There was no internet or social media back then, so it was personal and never seen by anyone who could pass judgment. All I knew was this: I enjoyed being creative, giving me an enormous sense of achievement. Whether or not I was good at the craft remained to be seen. I left school with average grades and fell into one job after another, not knowing what career path to take. One thing was certain: I wanted to settle down and have children someday, like most girls at that time, including my closest friends. I suppose writing wasn't viewed as a job to me then, and I had no university degree to boast about, which, I have since learned, isn't an essential requirement, but it does help. Sometimes we take the easy road in life because what we fear most is a failure. Believing this, my dream job was pushed aside for now.

My love for the arts remained strong, and I enjoyed various genres such as pop concerts, musical theatre shows, and movies. Observing the mastery of bringing a story to life and wishing on a star that I was just as talented.

Some years passed, and I did indeed get married and start a family, and amicably my husband and I agreed I would give up my job to raise our children. My life was complete, or so I thought. However, I still had a gnawing feeling of wanting to be creative and do something more. This stirred up mixed emotions, and I often thought, "I have responsibilities now" or "I'm not good enough."

Writing small pieces of poetry and painting on canvases filled my little spare time, being a full-time mum. During those early days of motherhood, we moved around a lot, and my husband was stressed to the hilt working all hours, barely even seeing the children. In addition, my extended family had issues of their own, which meant

I couldn't lean on them too much for support, and my eldest son suffered severely from infancy with eczema.

Watching my little boy suffer drained and saddened me. The toll was heavy, and I felt lost and helpless regarding the family's needs. My purpose was more about getting through each day instead of living for today. Questioning my own life, and beliefs, I wanted to find an answer, a way out for us all. There was a need for change, a word I had feared since childhood, but sometimes in life, we must face our fears and take a step in another direction for the greater good.

In 2007, we faced our biggest challenge, taking a giant leap of faith into the unknown. My husband and I immigrated to Australia with our two little boys. After seeing this extraordinary country, a couple of times—well, a small area of it at least—on holiday, we loved it!

They say, "You don't know what you've got until it's gone." Moving down under was my biggest sacrifice. Leaving my close-knit family and best friend, whom I'd known since I was 11, broke my heart. But I also knew we had to do it, and if it didn't work out, we could always move back. At that time, the purpose was to give our precious boys a great start in life. The salty sea air and ocean seemed to help with my son's eczema. Also, it was to support my husband's dream of owning a business. So, you could say we moved to a land of opportunities. The beach lifestyle and business venture soon paid off, meaning we could tick those boxes. Settling down in a new country took me a long time, but I felt it was the start of a new and prosperous future. Within a short time, the business grew, and we were the fortunate few who could afford to fly back regularly to visit our loved ones, but I still constantly felt the need to find my true purpose.

I met new and inspiring people that led me on a journey of rediscovery that required me to go deeper within myself and be more open-minded. So, I took up meditation and visualization and adopted the coaching method of 'The Law of Attraction'; I'm not a life coach per se; I just studied different areas of spirituality and embraced what resonated with me. I found it comforting and the results rewarding. I incorporate LOA into my daily routine, using meditation, a vision board, and affirmations.

By now, my boys were in full-time education, which freed up more of my time. I took advantage of the fact that I was still a stay-at-home-mum and joined various art classes, thinking I might sell pieces of art locally and keep fit by walking, playing tennis, or practicing yoga, but not all at the same time. It was a sampling phase, if you will, a chance to experience it all before I decided which felt best for me. Leading a more spiritual life helped alleviate past regrets, insecurities, and guilt in many ways. Faith is personal and deep, and the more I went within myself, as opposed to looking toward others to satisfy my needs, the less anxious I felt. The more I read, traveled, and participated, the more my mind expanded and invigorated my senses. Soon, travel became a major part of our lives, whether to different parts of Australia or unexplored nearby countries like beautiful Bali or revisiting England and touring new places with all its wonderful history.

These building blocks of life were fundamental in paving the way ahead for me. The results can be extraordinary when you do things with passion and a positive mindset. These cultural and visual experiences reignited my creative ideas for writing and, along with my love for music, would be the perfect recipe for inspiration. After a long period of no creative flow, I was somehow led back to writing.

Part three

One night, I woke up in my darkly lit bedroom from a dream, which was more like a message, as weird as that sounds. That dream was to change my path again, giving me the best story idea so far!

At this point, I had put all my creative writing on hold, but it shows that if it's your passion, you will be guided right back to it. Gradually, through my meditation and inspirational activities, a patchwork of ideas came streaming through. Paper and pen were my new accessories, and I wrote like a possessed woman most days. Even though I researched books on myths, knights, castles, and pirates, it was important to make the story authentic and my own. This was to be a historical fantasy, my first novel, and my biggest creative challenge yet. I wanted it to be my masterpiece or become a movie, so I visualized it. Escaping everyday life through my work became an obsession, and part of me never wanted it to end.

Finding a balance between home life and writing had its challenges, and yes, it's true, writers don't sleep much, either. Days turned into months, months turned into years, and to add to the mix, I gave birth to another beautiful son somewhere in the middle. Going through motherhood all over again took its toll; I was not as young as I was when I had my first two boys and constantly felt fatigued. Habitual sentiments crept back into my mind, guilt, unworthiness, failure, and homesickness. Still, through my reaffirming moments, I repeatedly told myself, "I am worthy." I remember being grateful to live in such a diverse and beautiful country as Australia and thankful for my healthy boys and loving husband. In the same breath, I could never forget my roots, family, and country of birth, dear old England. It will always have a place in my heart and my stories.

My writing went everywhere with me, on holidays, at picnics in the park with my boys, who were a great source of imagination for inventing characters, and even in shopping centers—if I saw a person who looked like a potential character for my story, they were going in it. From conception, my first novel took eight long years, mainly due to other commitments and inexperience. Nonetheless, my first manuscript was complete, and this was just the beginning. I had finally found my purpose—to be a writer!

Part Four

Rejection is not a word you want to hear when pursuing your dream. I kept going, though; after all, some of the great authors of our time were repeatedly refused, right? Only these "We regret to inform you" emails kept coming, and my spark of excitement was slowly fading. So, I took a break from the chase and focused on other interests. I devoted more time to my love of yoga, and during the lockdown, I would practice this ancient physical and spiritual activity daily. Then I said to myself, "What if this could be my dream job? My real purpose," and in 2021, I enrolled in a teacher training yoga course. The course lasted a whole year, and I thoroughly enjoyed it. Part of the course was to write and submit essay after essay and read numerous books on different areas of yoga; it awakened my love for writing more! I thought long and hard about what I could do to take charge of the situation. Analyzing every aspect, questioning, "Do I still believe in the story I wrote?" or "Do I need to improve on it?" I decided to go independent with this story. In the interim, I studied a few online tutorials from some of the best authors in the world. My mother always said, "You can never know too much," and she's right! Soon, I got to work on polishing my manuscript, feeling I had more to add or change, and I formed a book club to entice me back into reading—discipline and dedication were paramount. Once I ensured the manuscript was up to a better standard, I paused to save money for a professional editor, for marketing, and to learn more about my craft and the publishing world. All the while, I had no guru or mentor or agent to say, "You're doing the right thing." My gut feeling was my guide—and the internet, of course. If anything, this book has taught me patience, lots of it! Yoga helped me find my essence again, believe in myself, to grow, and trust in the plan.

A year later, I can hardly believe I'm writing this chapter in collaboration with other talented writers, feeling so grateful for the opportunity, not to mention the experience, while all going towards a great cause! By the time you read this chapter, I will have hopefully published my long-awaited fantasy fiction novel, *The Crystal Masters: Part One,* on Amazon, using my artwork and involving my love of history, magic, and adventure.

Sometimes the contradictions we face divert us to better outcomes or even a completely different path, one we may not have chosen ourselves.

To anyone wanting to follow their dream or find their purpose, don't wait for someone else to validate you.

Conclusion

Wouldn't it be nice to freeze time momentarily as we figure out our purpose? While that isn't yet possible, we can pause for thought and dream a little, or a lot, before taking action to set the wheels in motion, then wait patiently and watch everything unfold like a success story. I used to think, "I wish I had done this sooner," but I wasn't ready, knowledgeably, circumstantially, or financially. Looking back, I realize my life experiences have shaped and prepared me for the path I am on today. For me, it all happened at the right moment; for someone else, it could be an overnight revelation. By the time I reach my senior years, I hope to pass on more stories and words of wisdom, just like our older generation. To lead by example and not preach is my philosophy.

You may already know your purpose and are living it right now, in full swing. If so, great! People's paths are different, like no two snowflakes falling from the sky simultaneously have the same pattern or land. For those of you who just aren't sure, ask yourself, what makes your heart sing, your hairs stand on end, and your stomach churn with delight? What is it that drives you? I have constantly told my boys that I don't care what they do in life as long as it's something they love, whether choosing a job or a hobby. Like me, your purpose could be right under your very nose, and it might take a while to realize it, so be patient and be kind to yourself. You may never know your purpose or feel the need for one, and the answer could be just to be. One thing is paramount, follow your bliss, and when you know your purpose, don't hesitate because time waits for no one. Sure, there will be cloudy days when you can't see in front of you, but even clouds lift to reveal a brighter day. So, look up to the stars, grab the golden flares, and enjoy the ride!

I'll leave you with one of my favorite quotes; the author is unknown. However, it's one I can relate to, and I hope you can too, and that is, "Some people get lost in a forest while others find themselves there."

"Find a purpose in life so big it will challenge every capacity to be at your best."

~ David O. McKay

CHAPTER THREE

Discovering my Purpose

By Nadia Elmagrabi

"What does your gut say?" my mom asked. I was at a crossroads about which direction to go in life, so I asked my mom what she thought I should do. I was a teenager looking for guidance, and she returned it.

That was the moment she taught me that the answers lie within me. I remember feeling shocked and unsure about what "my gut" said. But it was at this moment that I realized that even my mother didn't know what was best for me and that only I could decide which path to take. In the years to come, I frequently returned to this advice whenever deciding which step to take next on my life path or what to eat for dinner.

After that moment, I reflected on what my body told me and learned how to listen. It took time and plenty of trial and error, but I eventually learned to trust it. If something didn't feel right in my body, my "gut," then I went in a different direction. Sometimes it would take me a while to heed the call, however. I remember being in a few relationships with boyfriends where within the first three months, my body told me this was not going to work. But I powered through and sometimes stayed in the doomed relationship for another two years before inevitably leaving.

The thing about tuning into my gut is that it doesn't always make sense. It's not logical, but it has always guided me to discover my purpose.

As a child, people always asked me what I wanted to be when I grew up. I had no earthly idea. I was completely blank to that question and thought something was wrong. I tried providing different answers, but I had no idea deep down. I remember asking my dad when he knew he wanted to be a doctor. He said he learned from the age of five. He always knew, and he lived his life according to that knowledge.

Growing up in Egypt, he attended medical school and practiced there until his mother died. Then he moved to the UK, met my mother, had two kids, and we moved to the United States. He had to do his residency again in both countries to practice, but he never flinched and just got it done. He knew what he wanted. I was envious of his deep knowledge and inspired by his fortitude and determination to overcome any obstacle that came his way to live the life he wanted for himself and his family.

Looking back on my relationship with my father, I see his influence more than ever on me discovering my purpose. He was committed to both his family and his patients. If anyone asked for his help with a medical concern, he was right there to do whatever it took to get them what they needed to get back on the road to health.

While my purpose isn't in the medical field, it is of service. My father's commitment to his patients and my mother's guidance in listening to my intuition influenced me to discover my purpose. But first, I had to find out what my purpose was not…

After high school, I went to a four-year university. I started out majoring in Fashion Merchandising. I love fashion and worked in retail for years during high school. I went with my classmates to Chicago for a fashion convention during the first semester and was blown away by how arrogant and cold people were. I had never felt so ignored and unwelcomed by a group of people. It was nothing personal, and I didn't take it personally; it was simply the event's vibe. Bleh. I hated it, and my body was repulsed by it all.

So that began my search for a new major. I changed it 8-10 times over the next four years. All along, while trying out different majors, I took classes that interested me most from teachers that I resonated with. I had one professor of Art History who was one such person. He was a genius and specialized in tribal art, particularly in the tribes of New Guinea. I didn't necessarily have an interest in tribal art, but what I learned in that class fascinated me, and I became very interested in the subject. Through the art of different indigenous tribes all over the planet through millennia, we can learn so much.

Tribes across the planet are organized in very similar ways. Their art is similar. They set up their living quarters like how they decide who marries who is similar. Everything about how they lived and their day-to-day life was similar. It blew my mind when I realized that tribes all over the planet lived following these same principles, yet they never communicated with one another. They used the stars as their guide and lived harmoniously with nature and their surroundings. They understood themselves as part of the universe and that their bodies held the universe within them. So Above, So Below. So Within, So Without. They lived according to the Laws of the Universe and knew these through observation.

I proceeded to take every class this professor taught. He was quite an asshole, but he was a genius, and I learned so much from him through art, including mathematics, physics, history, sociology, civilizations, and geography. I took so many of his classes that I ended up with a minor in Art History, even though that wasn't what I had set out to do.

The other subject I studied throughout college was French. I studied French in high school and loved everything about the nation and its culture. Then I spent a summer in Lyon with my classmates and loved every moment. The professors in that department were quirky and passionate about France, too, so it was easy for me to take those classes, and I got a major in French. Yet, I did not want to do anything, particularly with a French degree.

I dabbled in many other majors, including business and pre-med, both of which I nearly failed every class. I had no interest in those subjects and needed to care more to make myself do well in them. I wouldn't have gone to college if I had followed my gut during those years. I did it because that was what was expected of me by my parents, and I honestly didn't have any other thoughts about what I should have done. Since I did find myself in college, I tried to study practical subjects and major in something that would set me up for a "good future." But unfortunately, or fortunately, I could not make myself do something that I had no interest in.

I discovered a massage school near campus during my last year of college. I was intrigued and took a weekend course introducing me to massage therapy and basic techniques. No one I knew was doing this, and at the time, in the early 1990s in Western Michigan, massage was primarily associated with the erotic massage places off the side of the freeway. This was different. It was a therapeutic massage, and something about it appealed to me. I loved the classes, my connections with other students, and what I learned. I practiced with some of my friends, and it awakened something new within me.

During this time, two books jumped out at me in a used bookstore with my mom. One was a book about the life of Edgar Cayce, and the other was Perfect Health by Deepak Chopra. I had such *aha!* moments while reading these books. I resonated deeply with reincarnation after taking an Asian Literature class in college, and Cayce's teachings helped to anchor this understanding in my system. Perfect health showed me how we are different and unique and how what's right for one person might not be for another. I incorporated many of the practices he taught in that book and started to pay more attention to how I nourished my body and mind. Both books helped me understand that I oversaw my destiny and that it was up to me to take responsibility for myself and find my way.

After college, I spent time in Europe with family and friends and then moved to San Francisco to learn how to teach English as a second language. I planned to go to Japan to teach English when a friend living in Boulder, CO, called me, saying he needed a roommate. I was aimless then and had a full-body YES when he asked me to join him. Another friend joined me, and we moved. Still trying to decide what direction to go with work, I did temporary jobs in medical offices and food service at the stadiums in Denver.

I was considering going back to school for nursing and gained much clarity working at an alternative doctor's office. The doctor practiced a combination of Western and Eastern medicine, which was right up my alley. It was a busy office. I worked the front desk with a couple of other women. The nurses were SO busy; from what I saw, they spent most of their time doing paperwork. They had short visits with patients and went from one task to the next without much of a break. They seemed overwhelmed. It felt stressful and ineffective. It was not appealing, and this was supposed to be a holistic office. Once again, my body said NO.

I was clear that I wanted to work with people and do some healing work, and this was when I remembered my experience with massage therapy. Massage therapy in Colorado was much more common and considered an acceptable vocation than in Michigan at the time. And I would work directly with clients. So, I moved to Denver and enrolled in the Massage Therapy Institute of Colorado. I got a job at Le Central - The Affordable French Restaurant, and loved it all. I met amazing people at both places. I could walk or bike to school and work and felt at home.

I was on the right track regarding what to do for work. I loved doing massage and received great feedback. It was nourishing for the people I worked with and for me. During this time, I began my regular yoga practice and received ten sessions of Structural Integration from one of my teachers. Learning massage therapy, tuning into my body with yoga, and receiving this intense bodywork was a trifecta that helped me get tuned into my physical body and how it worked. I learned how to move more optimally, I learned how to tune into my physical body, and I used it to guide me in my healing. Finally, I shed layers of conditioning during this period and tuned into myself more than ever.

After finishing school, I moved to Telluride, CO, and became a massage therapist. Since childhood, I have envisioned living in the mountains, and now I am doing it! It felt surreal. For the first time, I moved somewhere by myself. I no longer had friends or family with me. It was tough, and some hard lessons showed me who I was and how to find the people I could trust and depend on. I loved my work and continued taking more bodywork classes, primarily Shiatsu and Reiki. I studied nutrition and Qi Gung and spent a lot of time hiking and snowboarding. I was never a hardcore snowboarder like a lot of the people there. I was much too cautious about that. I saw myself as someone who was there to support the hardcore people. They were the ones who benefited from the work I was doing. I felt aligned with my purpose when I was of service in this way.

One of the benefits of living and working at a ski resort is that there are months of "off-season" when the spa all but shuts down. So, I'd have a month or two off work every spring and fall. During that time, I'd travel. I grew up traveling to Europe, Egypt, and North America, visiting family, exploring, and continuing to travel during and after college. It was natural, easy, and so fun for me. I loved it and was compelled to travel during the off-season. I went to Southeast Asia, learned Thai massage, and then traveled around Cambodia and Vietnam. The adventure of travel lit me up and nourished my soul. I loved getting to know people worldwide and experiencing their cultures and food!

I used my intuition to guide me for every adventure I went on. For example, I wanted to spend time in Asia when someone I was working with at the spa said they were going to Southeast Asia for the off-season. I immediately lit up at the prospect, and she asked me if I wanted to go. It was a full-body yes for me. We ended up parting ways a few weeks in as we had different ideas about where to go after doing the massage program. It was perfect and allowed me to gain confidence in my ability to travel independently. I was rarely alone, as meeting like-minded travelers on the road was easy.

Another massage therapist I worked with in Telluride told me about her massage class on Kauai that combined structural integration, mindfulness meditation, and psychotherapy. Again, I was intrigued by what she said about her experiences, and again I was a full-body "yes" when she said she was going back and asked if I wanted to join her and do that training.

This training was pivotal as it further turned me into my mind, emotions, and spirit. During massage school in Denver, I became more aware of my physical body, where it was, and how it functioned in space. The mind/body connection was the missing piece for me, and the training in Kauai turned me onto how there's so much stored in our bodies, including memories, emotions, and trauma. I learned how to tune into, identify, and release energy from my body that was no longer serving me and facilitate this for others.

While living on Kauai, I connected with a community of people who were in ceremony with the land and followed traditional practices of sweat lodges and other ceremonies. I received deep healing during this time from participating in the sweat lodges alongside the healing work I was doing in the course. I shed layer upon layer of myself that forever changed the person I was when I arrived on that magical island. I was shown exactly where I was out of integrity in my thoughts, words, and deeds. I felt so transparent there and seen by those with whom I interacted. Seeing my vulnerability like that was confronting me in a way I had never experienced. There was no hiding from who I was. It was a humbling and enriching time.

The synchronicities and manifestations I experienced on the island were undeniable. One example was when I was with a couple of classmates, and we decided we wanted to go to the other side of the island. Just as we decided, a car pulled up and asked us if we needed a ride to the exact place we were going to. It was unbelievable. Nevertheless, I felt incredibly grateful to have that experience of living in such a magical place because it showed me what was possible.

And because everything flowed so succinctly, it felt like this was exactly where I was supposed to be. During this time, I had a vision of my true purpose. I was already living my purpose by following the breadcrumbs that led me to each of these experiences. It all felt very purposeful, even if the decisions seemed arbitrary or disconnected. I followed what lit me up, not knowing where I was headed, but I developed this deep trust that was like a compass within my body. I felt that something was right for me. It was a deep inner knowing. And when something wasn't right, my body contracted and moved away from whatever it was. Even if it were something my mind thought I wanted, sometimes my body would tell me a different story, and I learned to listen to my body more and more.

The vision of my purpose was to work with people holistically, incorporating the mind, body, and spirit. I was already on the path, and my next step was clear. I immensely enjoyed the psychology aspect and wanted to deepen my understanding. This was when I decided to go back to school for a master's degree in psychology as I continued to hone the physical and spiritual parts of myself and the work I was doing. I had never felt so clear; that vision still guided me.

I returned to Michigan after five years away, living a semi-nomadic lifestyle. It was a culture shock. It took me a while to orient myself back into the big city of Detroit. I applied to the Center of Humanistic Studies for their Master's program in Humanistic and Clinical Psychology. The program was experiential; we sat in a circle and processed a lot. It was the right fit for me. I was not looking for a rigorous mainstream academic experience but rather an environment where I could continue to immerse myself in the teachings and my healing. Again, I was guided to the perfect fit by following my intuition and the expansiveness I felt in my body when I first looked at this school.

I did my qualitative thesis on "What is the Experience of Becoming Balanced - Physically, Emotionally, Mentally and Spiritually?" I deduced from that work that becoming balanced is different for each of us. And balance for one person might have an emphasis on spirituality while another might have a focus on physicality. There's no perfect static balance; it's a fluid and changing experience. The balance can change at different times in our lives as we are focused on other areas. It is an active process that takes mindfulness, attention, and consideration to work on each area of life. When we change one area, the other areas are affected.

I began therapy for the first time during that program and eventually found my way to psychoanalysis. After I graduated and began practicing as a therapist, I knew that I had so much to learn to be effective, and part of that was continuing to do my inner work. I continued my studies at the Michigan Psychoanalytic Institute, where I received support from the analysts for the clients I was seeing. Again, it felt divinely orchestrated as I followed the breadcrumbs of my interests and what lit me up inside.

I continued practicing massage therapy and incorporated the embodiment practices with my clients that I learned in Kauai. During this time, I serendipitously met my husband on a Saturday afternoon at a frame shop. Something was different about him, and for the first time, I could see myself settling down with someone.

When we met, I still had the travel bug, but instead, I let go of my dream to travel to India to get married and eventually have children. My mother was thrilled that I was going to stay near her!

After having children, I became acutely interested in learning more about nutrition to help them and myself. There was so much conflicting advice about nutrition for children, and I wanted a more grounded perspective on it. My body felt out of whack after being pregnant or nursing for five years. I worked with a nutritionist to help me regain balance and went to school for health coaching. Again, I was motivated to learn how to help others as I was allowing myself. I could see that many of my therapy clients struggled with the day-to-day understanding of how to care for their health. I brought my new knowledge of how to heal the body with food into my client sessions to benefit them.

Slowly, my therapy practice transitioned into a hybrid of coaching and therapy. As I pursued my interests, I delved into the spirit world. I learned transcendental meditation and added that to my daily practices. I did more experiential healing work with a group of women focused on regenerating women's wisdom, which focused on healing the mother's and father's wounds for the benefit of the children of the earth.

Another serendipitous encounter at my dentist's office rekindled my interest in past-life therapy. As I talked with the office manager, we stumbled upon past lives, and she sent me a book called "Children's Past Lives," by Carol Bowman. I was lit up again and knew I wanted to learn more. I found Carol online and went to Philadelphia to train with her. Furthermore, it felt as if I was coming home and on the next right step of my path.

I was getting to the point with my work that I wanted to go deeper and connect directly with the subconscious mind to activate healing. Sometimes it felt like I got stuck with my clients; what they were conscious of was only part of the story, and I felt limited by traditional talk therapy. Past-life therapy was the answer to the prayer to get to a deeper layer of understanding around the source of what was keeping them stuck in unhealthy patterns and challenging relationships.

And, of course, past-life therapy contributed to my healing, too. During the first regression I experienced, I unlocked long-held grief and anger in my body that interfered with my relationship with my husband. I was astonished at the shift I felt in my body. I realized I was holding onto anger that I didn't know existed until I let it go. It was as if a huge weight was lifted off me, and as a result, my relationship with my husband deepened and blossomed in a way I didn't know was possible.

Past-life therapy has not disappointed me, as I have witnessed life-altering changes due to what my clients have discovered during a past life exploration. Due to our sessions, they often report feeling lighter, less anxious, more joyful, and more accepting of themselves and others. For example, one client woke up with intense anxiety every morning, and after our past-life session, it never happened again. Her energy was now free to focus on what she loved and wanted to create.

My latest deep dives are into Human Design and, most recently, Vedic Astrology. My Vedic chart shows that my dharma (purpose) is about healing from grief and helping others to do so, especially in relationships. Looking at all the ways I have worked with clients over the years, this makes so much sense. It is precisely what I have been doing. I hold space for them and their grief which is always around relationships. I have struggled with relationships over the years, and as I have healed my sisterhood wound and overcome challenges in my marriage, I help others do the same. Past-life work focuses on grief. Once we get to the root of our current issue by exploring a past life, there is always grieving to be done.

As I deepen into my purpose, I feel I'm slowing down. My life is simplifying. I am not interested in paying attention to anything unrelated to my family, close friends, work, or joy. Instead, I prioritize relationships with new and old friends that nourish my soul. I love to go deep and am grateful to have relationships with friends, clients, and mentors where we can explore the depths together. These relationships nourish my soul, and I love supporting my clients in deepening their most important relationships by acknowledging and honoring their grief.

My purpose intertwines with my healing. Whatever it is that needs healing in me is my guiding light, and in turn, I help others heal these parts within themselves. I have followed the breadcrumbs by tuning into my body and doing what lights me up. Each step has opened me up to the next one. It doesn't always make sense, but I have such a deep trust in my inner compass that I surrender myself. It has never steered me wrong.

We all have this inner compass and can know what is right by tuning into our bodies. It's like a muscle that needs to be exercised, and it's different for everyone. So, I encourage you to experiment with your inner compass and know that all you seek is within you.

“Be brave enough to live the life of your dreams according to your vision and purpose, instead of the expectations and opinions of others.”

~ Roy Bennett

CHAPTER FOUR

A Modern Woman's Tale of Finding Freedom, Liberation, and Purpose

By Renee Andreasen

As I write, I'm lying on black sand at Kahena Beach on the island of Hawaii, contemplating life and looking for inspiration for this chapter. A pretty good backdrop for writing, I'd say.

This beach was created during the explosion of Mount Kilauea in 1955. Then, in 1975 a major earthquake lowered the beach three feet and destroyed the stairs, making it even more challenging to get to. So, it's a hidden gem. A sacred place. Something only the curious and brave can access, just like you, finding your purpose.

I have several Hawaiian teachers who consider a volcano erupting a "remodeling" and the molten lava as raw, productive power (power is referred to as "mana" in Hawaiian) rather than a disastrous event. While it is true that the eruption destroyed jobs and homes, it is equally valid that it created new life and new beginnings. Like one's purpose, another is born when one aspect of a life's mission dies.

In case you've forgotten, the Earth is estimated to be between five and six billion years old. Our life span is 75 years, give or take, and right now, there are 7.8 billion people on the planet, with 385,000 babies born each day and 158,686 people dying each day. Please remember that these statistics are only as good as what is recorded, so there is a margin of inaccuracy. However, you get the point. It's a big planet, there are many people, and the size of the population is expanding and contracting constantly. Right now, on record, more people are being born than dying.

At this point, you may also be contemplating if the Earth is that old, if your life is this short, and if there are so many people, what is the point? Do I matter? Can I make a difference?

The answer is yes, of course you can. We are each born with a purpose to fulfill here on Earth.

Scientists consider "life" as plants, animals, bacteria, and fungi. These organisms, once alive, are now fossils found in rocks that we use to measure the planet's age. And explosions from volcanoes are considered "physical changes."

Imagine that to be considered a part of "life" in the planet's history, you've got to die and become a part of the Earth's crust. To be considered "life"—a physical change to the world—we need to exist, contribute to it, and then leave. The dinosaurs, for example, came and went billions of years ago. Their life and assimilation with the earth's crust resulted in the energy source, oil, that we depend on most and continually have wars over. Where would we be without the dinosaurs?

So, the question is, what is the contribution? What is one's purpose?

There is a current trend in being purposeful, finding one's purpose, and making a difference in the world. With so much exposure through social media and the visibility and accessibility of other lifestyles, it's easy to compare yourself to someone else. Surprisingly, I have talked with many people who have achieved much in this lifetime but are still unsure of or unsatisfied with their purpose. These people are CEOs of companies, doctors who save hundreds of lives, philanthropists, and owners of successful businesses.

One concrete example is someone I know whom I highly respect, who shared with me recently that they are unsure of and seeking life's purpose. This person has traveled the world saving starving children, owns five businesses, has a Ph.D., and opened an orphanage. One would think they've already found and completed their purpose ten times over.

I don't judge them. I celebrate them. Like the volcano and Kahena Beach, they are ready for a rebirth. They've outgrown who they were and what they accomplished, their belief system has changed, and they are prepared for something more. Through life, they have learned, conquered, and outgrown the person they were. The old self isn't "bad," and the new self isn't "good" or "better." They are all versions of ourselves that served a purpose for a time, helping us grow and learn from the experience of that time.

The collective souls of this planet, from past and present—like the fossils—are what create life consciousness and betterment of the Earth. Each generation brings wisdom from their life experience, leaving the legacy of their knowledge and expertise to their children and the people they impacted. Each generation brings us closer to reaching the ultimate potential of humanity.

One cannot go wrong in discovering their purpose.

Through my journey, I learned that my purpose is to teach others to heal themselves naturally and to help people lighten up and have more fun! I am also passionate about assisting pregnant mothers to keep their babies healthy so we can improve the health of Americans.

To discover all this, I went through my journey of struggling with pregnancy, becoming malnourished and bedridden, feeling scared, helpless, and at times hopeless and trapped. Through that journey to rebirth, I learned that my beliefs and actions could cause and cure illness. Through my healing, I realized that I could help others heal naturally, and it's become my passion and purpose.

The catalyst for significant change was spending ten days in silent meditation. That time alone, away from my daily life and routines, yet within the safety and structure of the program, gave me a chance to let go and be alone with my thoughts. It allowed me to be quiet, listen to my inner dialogue, and become aware of my thoughts and their origins. Over the ten days, I could see I was unhappy in my marriage, career, and belief system.

Sitting silently, I realized my mind and thoughts were very loud. I became acutely aware that I no longer wanted the life I had created for myself. I realized how unhappy I was. My mind, body, and spirit were slowly deteriorating. Until then, I was proud of my life: a successful, high-paying career, two beautiful children, a dedicated husband, a million-dollar home, and a healthy 401k. But was this my purpose? I felt I didn't fit into my old life anymore.

Six months later, Kahena Beach and Pahoa, Hawaii, became my next version of the silent meditation retreat. I was there for six months instead of ten days. I lived off-grid, where cell phones didn't work very well. We slept with the moon, rose with the sun, and occasionally looked at clocks. It's easy to lose track of the day and the date. The only things that exist are what you're experiencing in each moment, who you're with, what you see, and whatever is on your mind and body, the latter of which is optionally clothed.

This sacred black sand beach is a beautiful container to host a community of unique beings, locals, strays, spiritual knowledge seekers, eccentric artists, musicians, dancers, and tourists. It's unique and different from your average beach, and people arrive open-minded. As you remove your layers of clothing, you strip away your ego. People come here to feel and be free. It's where people play like children and have fun like no one is watching. Most people come to this beach and this city to find a purpose or to escape. You don't end up here by accident; this place attracts unique people looking for that sacred place.

Topics of discussion center around the meaning of life, spiritual beliefs, how to change the world, and what you dream for the planet.

When you meet someone, you don't ask them their name. Instead, you ask them what they call themself. Answers run the gamut from Sunshine Spirit to Jsemal and the occasional Frank. The last thing you discuss is what you do for a living and how you make money. Instead, people tell you or ask you about the meaning of life.

I often come to this island and this beach because it is where I can be free and clear my mind. Freeing my mind and detaching from traditional society gives me time to pause, learn new ways of thinking, and decide what to do with that information. I also find that being in nature and surrounded by creatives gave me a chance to relax and reconnect with my purpose fully.

Over the past ten years, I have overcome a significant health crisis where I was bedridden twice and learned about healing naturally. While healing and recovering myself, my son was also diagnosed with an autoimmune disease and became bedridden. When I was at the beach and starting this chapter, I was recovering from ending my 21-year marriage, building my own wellness company, and repairing my relationships with my children. I needed a break from it all. Hawaii and freedom are my medicine.

I'm going through a rebirth at the graceful age of forty-nine. Almost two years ago, I liberated myself from a twenty-one-year marriage and quit my corporate day job to travel the world for a year and work for myself. My time in corporate gave me some money to work for myself and build a wellness company. I love my company; however being an entrepreneur is a lot of work, so I may change my mind, get re-married, and work for someone again for medical benefits and college tuition for my children if needed. If I do, it will be of my own free will and choice versus something I just fell into.

I came to Hawaii with the intent to release my roles and attachments and be of service to the Universe. While that was my intent, I wasn't exactly sure how to do it. I came here with my thirty-year-old lover and best friend, seventeen years my junior, as an act of escape and exploration. We had a wild love affair. Against all odds of us living 2,500 miles apart, we met on a beach walk at sunrise on Venice beach the day after I escaped from my husband and cried myself to sleep asking the Universe for love. We quickly became deeply connected, expressed love for each other the first night we were intimate, then flew home separately, wondering what had just happened.

His mission was to be pure love to all and service to his family. When he met me, he switched his focus from his family to me while we were together. This was a new concept for me. To be loved. It was magical; I became entranced. We flew back and forth from Ohio and Seattle for a few months, then decided he would join me on my travels to Hawaii.

Barely knowing each other, we became inseparable and lived together at a meditation and ecological center in a mostly screened hut at a retreat center in the jungle alongside wild pigs and croaking frogs that were so loud you couldn't sleep. We worked in exchange for rent and food. The meditation center is off-grid, generating solar power and capturing water from rain. Fresh fruits and vegetables are grown on the property, and we mostly ate and lived off the land.

I went from the boardroom to the bathroom, cleaning toilets and changing beds for upcoming guests. I became a listening ear and surrogate mother, and counselor for the young world travelers who came to this part of the island on their journey to discover their purpose. I tried to give more than I took emotionally and shared wisdom when asked. I had to remind myself that I wasn't a mother, manager, or leader each day. Instead, I attempted to be a servant of the Universe and a giver who gladly does what the community needs without complaining.

I did my best not to share too much of my story and be whatever was needed: prep cook, housekeeper, trusted advisor, or driver. But, at times, it was difficult to surrender to the purpose of putting all others above myself, and I made many mistakes. I also found that suppressing my personal needs conjured up feelings of entrapment from my childhood, marriage, and corporate employment.

I gained insight into what matters to people by offering my time and attention. I learned what I value versus what others value and what matters to the community and the planet. Through observation, I realized that people are creative and limitless. Yet, many are lonely and don't feel fully seen, heard, or understood. I learned that the planet is far more resilient than we think, and while it is delicate, it will also create balance and authority through a hurricane, flood, or volcanic eruption.

The wisdom I gained that I value most is that making money doesn't matter to many people. Instead, they see riches as freedom, creativity, community, and being close to nature. It has changed my understanding of success and abundance, and I will never see money the same way again.

What's interesting about having extended time with a purpose of service and exploration resulted in clarity on how I'd like to align my purpose. It became clear that I want to be productive, but only if I do something I like or believe has value. I could see that while I was a productive person in my former life, I didn't believe in the value of what I was doing or how I was contributing towards that meaning. I was moving through life without conscious awareness of my decisions, mostly based on survival tactics, promotion requirements, and materialism. I had fallen into traditional societal beliefs and familial patterns that women like me typically fall into.

In many moments of what felt like an escape in Hawaii, I was full of guilt and confusion because of all I had left at home. Now, I see things more clearly and celebrate the courage and creativity it took to build a new life not on just my terms but the terms of the Universe, as a catalyst for me to connect with my true purpose. Being there, being naked and free, changed everything. The relationship ended a few months after returning to the mainland when I settled back into working, focusing on my new life, self and expanding my business. There were too many miles, years, and life experiences between us to sustain what we had created in Hawaii. I cherish that time and who we were, and I will lock the experience in my heart forever. I am grateful for all I learned through love and adventure.

The privilege of a lifetime is to become who you are. Through my experiences and learnings, I realized I have been following a universal process toward discovering my purpose, which falls into the following awareness elements.

The Awakening

It's fair to say I had an awakening. My counselor told me that's what was happening to me about a year before I meditated in silence. The awakening started when I realized my belief system wasn't my choice but the one that my job, family, and society rewarded me for. I realized I had been living a life that made others happy and me miserable. I lived to make others happy, and most weren't that happy. It seemed silly and no longer worth my time when I realized this.

I became sick after attempting to reach unrealistic expectations and making other people happy. It was hard to justify continuing that path.

Life traumas triggered my sickness, which manifested into anxiety and autoimmunity. My body made it very clear that what I was doing was no longer sustainable or healthy and began attacking itself as if I were the disease.

There was no pharmaceutical medicine to cure what I had. If I didn't change, I might die. I learned that, while uncomfortable, life had a way of leading me toward my purpose.

Exploration of spirituality and the meaning of life

My ten-day meditation and time in Hawaii led me to a Hawaiian elder who helped me dive deep into the teachings of Hawaiian mysticism and Shamanic ways. She also helped me discover Tantra, Hinduism, meditative yoga, and chanting. Developing spiritual rituals and a deeply meditative practice helped me uncover my understanding of life and spirit and how I now see the meaning of life and the Universe.

I was spiritually cleansed, initiated, and blessed in Hawaiian and Hindu lineages. I didn't even know these things existed as I was raised a Christian. This was so far removed from the path of my childhood, yet it seemed right.

By forgiving myself for the past and learning that I was pure and worthy of love without forgiveness, I permitted myself to release guilt and attachments to the past and any associated shame. I blossomed once I opened myself up to the possibilities of what could exist outside my traditional training, knowledge, and experience.

Prioritization of values

I recognized the value of others and realized that my community, my children, and how I treated people and the planet were critical for me to live a fulfilling life with purpose. I value creativity, freedom, and playing. Contributing to society and bettering the world through honesty and love of the planet is paramount.

Other ways to do this are to identify and prioritize one's values, rank and score them, and then compare your actions to your priorities to see how aligned you are. I do this every few months to further clarify what is important to me. Each time I do this, it reveals how aligned I am with my values and if I need to close the gap.

Closing the gap between your values, beliefs, and actions helps you get closer to discovering your purpose. The more you align your beliefs and activities, the easier things become because you stop working against yourself, and your purpose is often revealed.

Discovering natural gifts and talents

The best way to do this is through exploration and play. You can be more open-minded when the stakes are low, and your income or assets are not on the line. Going big and experimenting with what you've always wanted to do lets you determine if the fantasy is close to reality. The longer you think about something, the longer you delay knowing the truth. We only know what we are naturally good at by trying it. So, the doers do, and the wishers wish. Unfortunately, wishing does not bring purpose.

In my case, at the beginning of my awakening, my stakes were high. I was sick and wasn't getting better. Healing was not optional, and I needed an answer. I researched solutions and tested them on myself. I learned what worked and what didn't by how it affected my energy. I followed the things that increased my energy and made me feel happy.

Later, when my body healed, I took courses in health and wellness that explained what I had done. Rather than learning through desperation, I was able to slow down and learn the method and science behind it.

Purpose through struggle and experience

Now, as my body is healed and my mind is sharp, I can explore and play with eccentric and ancient ideas through a creative process where my life is no longer at stake. I'm now in a phase of expansion and teaching others what I have learned, and it's gratifying to see others regaining their body, lives, and minds. To see others regain their health, vitality, and soar makes my struggle worth everything I went through.

I am now pursuing a PhD in Natural Medicine. I turned my crisis into science, transforming my experiences into teaching opportunities, which became my purpose. Most recently, I've added vibrational and sound healing to my skillset. When I worked in corporate management, I couldn't imagine this would become my life's calling. It's amazing what comes your way when you're open to it.

Mastering the mind and evolving

None of us is perfect, and we are constantly perfecting. As you go through this process, refrain from judging who you are and how well you're doing. Evaluating your effectiveness is different from judgment.

Mastery takes time, perseverance, and practice. Learning from our past and looking at our pitfalls can be alarming. While self-mastery and finding purpose are an inner journey and one traveled on your own, I realized that by informing your friends and family you are changing, they are more receptive and may help you on your journey. Others will not know what you went through; they see the results, ask you what you're doing, and want a piece of what you've got.

The good news is that as you gain experience, alignment, and mastery become easier and can happen faster. As you build a community more aligned with your purpose, it becomes easier to find support. It becomes less disruptive and more graceful. When you get good enough at change, you earn the right to teach others your process, and what you went through so they can do it too.

For me and many others, creating awareness of the self and discovering your purpose can require pain. And loss. But also joy, liberation, and pleasure. Discovery and adventure. I like to think the pain and loss I went through is what makes it interesting. "Grit to work with," one of my mentors called it. I didn't wake up one day knowing my purpose; discovery is dynamic and unpredictable.

Each tweak or major overhaul changed my thoughts, beliefs, and language. How I thought about things, saw things, and talked about these things changed. The words and actions I chose had outcomes and consequences. It affected the people around me. They either loved it, hated it or were neutral. As my behavior and decisions changed, people formed opinions about my changes. They were either comfortable with it or uncomfortable with it. Those who were uncomfortable separated from me, or I separated from them, and I also attracted new people and environments as I changed. I attracted things in harmony with where I was headed—my purpose.

I also like to believe that the size of my rebirth equates to the greatness I will experience in this lifetime. Greatness isn't defined as me and my ego, my legacy, or who I become and what I accomplish, but rather, the journey of sorrow, joy, pleasure, fun, and the people I meet and influence along the way. I am also experiencing the greatness of the people who come into my life and share their experiences. The road to purpose is a two-way street; everyone travels it together.

As we grow and increase our consciousness and expand ourselves, it becomes easier to connect with and have compassion for others and appreciate their points of view. It helps to build empathy and connection with the planet and humanity. In my world travels the most common thread is that people believe their purpose in life is to become pure love. Overwhelmingly, this is the common truth I've heard from interviewing hundreds of people who don't know each other.

It's beautiful. If a loss occurs to become love, one must let go of anger, hate, blame, and shame to become and spread love.

Forgiveness, detachment, and compassion help one become more aligned with their purpose even if they can't label or define it clearly.

The purpose which you're fulfilling changes as everything changes: your living conditions and your environment change. The people around you change. Old things end, and new things begin. Nothing is lost, and everything is gained, and your journey and purpose become a part of the history and evolution of humankind.

You create a new life and new beginning every day of your life. Stay true to yourself, have some fun, loosen your grip, and leave a little bit to chance so that you're always an adventure.

Like the dinosaurs and the volcanos, it takes time for your true purpose to reveal itself. The possibilities for your life are endless, and you are the only one in charge of writing your story.

"You don't decide what your purpose is in life you discover it. Your purpose is your reason for living."

- Bob Proctor

CHAPTER FIVE

Life Purpose

By Marie Chandler

The year was 2005. I was new to Australia, having relocated from the Netherlands, and attending an event, keen to network with other women in IT. The theme of the evening's presentation was the difference between a job and a career. I was looking forward to some pearls of wisdom and learning from the different speakers' life experiences. A job is simply trading your time for money. A career is when you have aspirations, a vision, and a long-term purpose.

It was a good evening, nothing earth-shattering until the final speaker talked about a job, a career, and a life purpose. Her presentation kickstarted my journey to question everything in my life. My head was full of existential questions - Why was I here? – Not in the room with amazing women, but what was my purpose in this lifetime? What have I achieved? What legacy do I want to leave, and to whom? And so, it began.

I'd already committed to learning new ways to improve my communication skills because I often felt misunderstood. I could see things other people didn't notice, and I was passionate about things no one cared about. Until now, my life choices seemed to be about living life to the fullest, having fun, and traveling; now, I felt it was time to focus on my career. My next career choice needed to be purposeful. But where to begin? Thus began the quest to discover my purpose.

By December 2022, I'd written a book chapter on motivation in the *Journey of Riches* book series, and John had invited me to write a chapter in a book on finding your life purpose. I laughed – Did I want to go there again with my writing? Did I want to add some stress to my life? I'd just renovated my kitchen, which had been somewhat stressful; I wanted 2023 to be more about ease and grace. I asked him if I could have a few days to think about it. For three days, I asked myself, "What is my life purpose?" "Have I found my life purpose?" "What does it even mean?" After three days, I had my answer: I couldn't answer any of those questions, so I'll write the chapter. Knowing who I am and what I'm like, I'll demystify those questions and trust the process. Challenge Accepted.

I sat down to brainstorm, looking back on my life, and I could easily see how my life purpose differed in each decade. However, upon reflection, I saw some patterns in my life, strange moments, and brief encounters. What has inspired and challenged me? I started to ask people, "Have you found your life purpose?", "Are you living your dream?", "Are you still seeking?", " What about your friends – what do you notice?"

Some clear themes emerged. Some people seem connected to their life purpose from a very young age; they are laser-focused, and every decision is based on achieving that mission. We all know people like that. Take Gandhi, for example. As a child, he never hit back. He challenged the caste system by touching the untouchables and was inspired by a play about Harishchandra, a King who was famous for his love of truth. His education in England trained him to be a barrister, and the opportunity brought him to South Africa. Gandhi's first success as a lawyer was not a crushing victory over an opponent but a triumph of good sense and humanity. The theme of his life-fighting injustices earned him the title of Mahatma (Sanskrit for "Great-Souled"). I love people who know their purpose and can shape their decisions accordingly. It reminded me of Steven Covey's "7 Habits – Lesson 1" - Begin with the end in mind.

Other people seem to be clear on a path until a curve ball happens, something major that drives change, such as an accident, a breakdown, or a change of heart, which forces them to reimagine, refocus and take the necessary steps. The door has been closed firmly shut, not to be opened again.

Such is the case with Anita Moorjani. Anita was born in Singapore, moved to Sri Lanka, and ended up in Hong Kong. Tri-lingual and of Indian descent, living in Chinese society. Educated in a British school, she knew from a young age that she did not want to be a traditional Indian housewife. She quickly rose through the ranks in the financial industry, relocating to Paris, France, when the global financial crisis hit in 1997. Through a stressful period, she reinvented herself as a cultural, corporate trainer helping ex-pats integrate into Hong Kong living.

In 2002 life gave her a new challenge when doctors discovered that she had lymphoma. Refusing traditional cancer treatment, she journeyed inwards. A lifetime of people-pleasing had taken its toll on her; in 2006, she experienced an NDE (Near Death Experience). In her book "Dying To Be Me" she shares her out-of-body experience. She is now an accomplished author and inspirational trainer. She inspires me to trust my intuition on what is best for me, and I love that she allowed doctors and scientists to measure, probe, and pontificate on how this seemingly impossible event occurred. This resonates with my goal of integrating Western medicine with Eastern philosophy.

Many people spend much time thinking and fantasizing, yet they fail to act. Others never even ponder their life purpose; they seem content to just go with the flow. Some people discover their purpose through fulfilling their passions and interests, and others aspire to impact the world through work or volunteering positively; others choose to raise a family.

Whatever you choose, make sure that it ignites a spark within you so that you can sustain that energy. You may live in harmony with nature, achieve inner peace and calm, or contribute to society by being of service. In a nutshell, this is not about comparing your life choices and circumstances with others. This is about you becoming you and choosing whatever ruffles your truffles and sizzles your bacon. Whether you pursue a sense of adventure, seek spiritual enlightenment, engage in personal growth and development, or positively influence others - choose what makes you happy, what stimulates you, and what will bring you joy.

I am inspired by "The Man of La Mancha" – The Impossible Dream (The Quest). My life has always been about dreaming the impossible dream and reaching the unreachable star.

In retrospect, I've always been the eternal student, the seeker of knowledge, and I seek to lift others when possible. Since 2005 I have studied various disciplines to discover my life purpose. In my corporate life, I grew a team, learned about corporate leadership and organizational structure, and became qualified as a CSM (Certified Support Manager). I needed to build and nurture a challenging and growing team while preparing them for their next roles based on their personal goals, drive, and aspirations.

My team achieved 100% customer satisfaction because we sought to understand what was important for our customers and personalized their experiences. As a result, I was invited as a Support winner to the Sales Club Excellence in Borneo (the first support manager in the history of Oracle to be so honored) to celebrate our success, which was a fabulous acknowledgment of all we'd achieved that year.

I was driven to be a better communicator and to resolve my inner conflicts, struggles, and insecurities that weren't obvious to others. They only noticed my confident and courageous exterior – these days, it would be labeled imposter syndrome. I set crazy goals and accomplished them, yet the empty feeling inside was never quite fulfilled. I have explored, considered, and researched several topics and techniques. Some use the logical brain and question science, while others focus more on pseudo-science and metaphysics. I sought insights through astrology (relating human behavior to the movement and alignment of planets and how this influences the individual).

I was born on the cusp of Libra and Scorpio, which means that I essentially strive for balance and equanimity and, like the scorpion, can have a sting on my tail.

I scrutinized where I was willing and woeful and sought mentors, coaches, and therapists who would support, challenge, inspire, break, and rebuild me. I stepped up to do the work and became conscious that I was playing too small, remaining within my comfort zone. I looked back at all the times I'd failed and saw that I always got back up again. Instead of beating myself up, I started to recognize my internal resources. I became aware of my potential to keep growing. I learned to be comfortable with being uncomfortable. I sought opportunities to challenge myself and fail and grow from the experience. I developed resilience and lived with purpose. By 2012 I'd become a trained coach, hypnotherapist, face reader, and Psychosomatic Therapist and realized that my next learning opportunity would be to share that knowledge as a teacher. I am amazed by the students and clients I've attracted to ensure my learning always takes an upward trajectory.

After four years of teaching, it was time to become a student again in new and different arenas. I firmly believe that we must evolve as our purpose evolves. So, I attended psychic development classes looking for explanations for some inexplicable and intolerable experiences I was enduring. Concurrently, I studied for my Cert IV in Training and Assessments. My greatest takeaway from that year was that some teachers enlighten you, whereas others illuminate what not to do and how not to be. This taught me one of my greatest lessons, the art of discernment, and sharing this with clients takes them to the next level of purposeful living.

In March 2017, an opportunity to walk the Camino De Santiago arrived. The Camino is also known as The Way of St James, a traditional pilgrimage; it starts at St. Jean Pied de Port in France and ends at the Santiago de Compostela in Galicia, Spain (home to the tomb of St James). My role at work became redundant, and just like that, my time at Vantive, PeopleSoft, and Oracle ended. My 800km journey was just around the corner—my real purpose was to challenge the principles of Psychosomatic Therapy and experience a mind-body connection. Being in tune with the body and allowing the body to find its rhythm. I walked the Camino, traveled around Europe, spent time in the UK, and enjoyed three months in America.

Those nine months created spontaneous opportunities to bring face reading to different corners of the globe. I wanted some curious mystical and magical experiences opening my mind to possibilities that could not have been planned. The experience allowed me to release control, trust the universe and be open. In the words of Lewis Carroll, "If you don't know where you're going, any road will get you there." As a result, my life purpose continues to unravel before me; similar to cross stitch and wool, it's in the disentangling that you reach a point when you become ready to create your next masterpiece.

During the Camino, I gained clarity on when I was thrilled. It was when I moved to the Netherlands post my around-the-world trip.

My colleagues were my friends, the job was both challenging and rewarding, and I was constantly learning and could envision where I'd like to be in five years. I wanted that again but wasn't sure it was possible. Was I naïve in my mid 20's? Could this be possible to achieve in my mid 40's? What did I not know then that I know now? What did I know then that I now believe I was wrong about? What was I willing to change? What was I willing to accept? I also loved the opportunity The Camino offered me. I read hundreds of faces along the way and had many deep and meaningful conversations, reflections, realizations, and revelations.

According to my Psychosomatic fellow teachers, one of my gifts and skills is helping people find their life purpose and guiding them to identify and acknowledge their skills and the perfect job according to their facial structure and facial features. As one's biography is written all over their face, the impressions on your face show where your preferred tendencies lie, and I shine a spotlight on these.

My face had changed significantly; my mind and body were newly synchronized, and I was internally stronger, more self-aware, and connected. Once back In Sydney and pondering my next steps, I spent two weeks on a cruise as the enlightenment speaker as we sailed around New Zealand. I gained real clarity during that cruise that my life purpose is an amalgamation of being of service in both my working life and volunteering pursuits, as well as a mix of goal setting, planning, and divine interventions to enjoy explorations, adventures, and pilgrimages along the way.

With the cruise completed, the next learning and development phase was evident. My life purpose was to gain an ever-deeper understanding of Psychosomatic principles in health. First, I wanted to expand my understanding of Psychosomatics as a new medical field in comparison and contradiction with conventional approaches to healing. Second, I sought opportunities to spend time with medical researchers to dive deeply into my familial medical history. Finally, I pursued various research studies into brain development, dementia, the impact of stress on the nervous system, and sleep, memory, and cognition tests. I was open to this new self-healing paradigm instead of more conventional approaches.

I spent hours of conversations with medical researchers, comparing empirical data with anecdotal evidence of my lived experiences and various clients I have seen. We discussed emotional anatomy, unresolved emotions in disease causation, and the interrelation between body systems and dysfunction. I was comparing the results of my MRI brain scans, x-rays, blood test, and sleep study aligned with my psychosomatic history (a diary of accidents, incidents, and operations) and current medical conditions. I could consequently map the effects on my physiology and health to emotional triggers and unresolved conflict in my past to disease causation.

I used this information also to map it to anecdotal evidence of my clients, and this experience deepened my purpose and passion for helping others to a level beyond what I thought was possible.

During that time, slowly but surely, I became more aware of my self-worth, and I became aware of my potential. My confidence increased, and my client's results improved. I also wanted to continue to grow. I got slapped down, rejected, ridiculed, and retrenched various times, and each time, I rebuilt with a stronger foundation. Like the story of the three little pigs, I had more resources and wisdom each time I rebuilt and constructed more solid foundations I could build upon.

I realized that my firm foundations come from recognizing my uniqueness and what makes me different by allowing that to be ok. I no longer sought approval from outside of myself. I had changed from dependence to independence, and I knew that the next step was interdependence – I wanted my clients to believe that their dreams could be achieved, and I wanted to coach them to get there. I knew I could coach, share, support, and facilitate, but it was solely (soul-ly) up to them. They are responsible for their results. I watched my clients transform before my eyes.

As I connected with my clients on a deeper level and they came to trust me, they reconnected with their bodies, and amazing things started to happen. They resolved long-held issues in the tissues. In February 2023, I studied with Bessel van der Kolk, author of *The Body Keeps The Score*, discovering innovative ways to work with clients and assist them on their healing journeys. My additional in-depth studies continue to reaffirm the importance and validity of Psychosomatics as a pioneering method still unfolding. In addition, realizing how much I play devil's advocate, I saw the positive benefits of reminding people whom they are, supporting them on their journey, and helping them find direction when they feel lost. I reconnect my clients with their bodies; I help them see where they have been out of alignment. This provides a baseline on which they can strengthen their foundations; with that secure base, they feel safe to explore their purpose further.

I'm the first person to believe in some of my clients and their abilities. I remind them who they are. I give them the courage, encouragement, and permission to chase their dreams, follow their desires, and choose themselves for the first time. I champion my clients to set valiant goals and actively support and uplift them. When we put ourselves first, our purpose finds us. Retrospectively I think about when people believed in me even when I didn't believe in myself. I also think about those who didn't believe in me when I believed in myself. I muse over people who ridiculed and challenged me, not to dissuade me but to bring me down so they could lift themselves. This only made me more driven to discover and live with purpose.

I reflect on people who've been my teacher, not because of who they taught me to be but by teaching me who I don't want to be. I may have lost momentum sometimes, but I rarely failed to learn the lesson. When I did, the scenarios showed up again. There were different actors but always the same narrative until I allowed the ideas to spark, lighting the eternal flame that radiated my soul. The most fundamental part of working with others is to develop their trust, and when you're seeking your life purpose, you need to trust the process. You need to trust that you are exactly where you're meant to be and that the right people will cross your path at exactly the right time, be they perpetrators, impersonators, and circuit breakers. Each experience will challenge you on a deeper level to trust the process.

I've learned lessons and what I think is important to share. Firstly, as soon as you grasp new skills, cement those learnings by teaching them to someone else. It will highlight your gaps, and you will have mastered the skill. Know yourself and revel in who you are. Some people like to live in their comfort zone. Not everyone is willing to try to rise, emerge, elevate, and grow. I'm constantly curious; I will find out if I don't know something. Spiritual growth is not always love and light. Sometimes, it can be blood, sweat, and tears, as you must be willing to unlearn what you know to learn something new. You must be ready to say no, to walk away, and to be able to sit with uncomfortable feelings. You have to feel the emotions to be able to process them, and in turn, it is only through this awkward process that those feelings dissipate.

Helping people uncover, discover, and rediscover their life purpose inspires me. Each client comes in for unique reasons. The first session is always a face reading – so they can visually see where they are today (it is essential to have a baseline). Your biography is written all over your face. You'll discover your masculine and feminine tendencies and influences, the percentage of each, and whether you're in conflict or collaboration with yourself. You'll also identify your preferences regarding your mental, emotional, and physical approaches. We focus on each feature and the inter-relational impacts and effects they have. During the last part of the reading, you will receive your photo splits—a visual representation of your masculine and feminine internal responses to external experiences.

The client always decides what is next for them. This information is sufficient for some as they already have the resources and support networks. Some choose the coaching package to work through their obstacles and perceived limitations. Others select coaching to build upon their strengths. A small percentage of people feel ready to delve even deeper. We complete a full psychosomatic assessment to review operations, accidents, and incidents that have left an indelible imprint on their life.

The stepping stones of the past provide the pathway to the future. Connecting the dots resolves emotional blockages and releases the stuck energies in the body. Deeper insights give the key to unlocking future potential. When you fully connect to the deeper unconscious, this is where you discover your hidden purpose.

Some people know their life purpose and have no doubts, others accidentally find their life purpose, and others find that their purpose finds them. When you don't have a clear vision, blindly taking that next step reveals the path. When faced with challenges, it's an opportunity to choose and discern whether now is the time to overcome that challenge or sit back and allow things to unfold, trusting the process. You will not be everyone's cup of tea; not everyone is ready to face their fears. In my coaching and teaching business, I help individuals and teams discover their purpose, nurture their mindset, and align with their intentions. I work with people to bridge the gaps and close the great chasm that may make them afraid. Just as I did in my corporate life, working in cyber security, I protect people and defend data, only now I work with minds instead of machines.

You can't just plant a seed and expect a flower to appear magically; there must be time to process. The seed needs to germinate. A chick isn't just born; the egg needs to be incubated. A hamster takes a month to gestate, a human nine months, and a whale takes over a year. So how long does it take for thoughts to be actioned? When we think about life's purpose, how quickly does it happen? We need to plan and act! We also need time for thoughts to incubate, ideas to germinate, and goals to gestate. Sometimes you need to rest and recuperate; other times, you must be consciously aware that you are heading toward a growth spurt. Let your spirit inspire you, allow yourself time to discover your talents, and be mindful of what you can control and influence and what you need to let go of.

Identify people in your sphere whom you can help and be open to receiving help yourself. Above all – trust that you can always develop new skills and abilities. It is up to you to identify your dreams and aspirations and to address your obstacles and limitations. Aim to be open to learning and be teachable. Identify the difference between a stretch goal and when to ask others for help. Help others and recognize where you are being stubborn. When you fail - Remind yourself that you have found another way that doesn't work for you, so you're one step closer to your desired outcome. Speak to yourself as you talk to others – Be kind and patient. Allow time to learn, grow, ask for help, and acknowledge how far you have come.

If you're seeking or pursuing your life purpose, you can travel and have external people experiences or journeys within. If you feel alone, seek opportunities to connect. Say hi to people at the bus stop. Seek opportunities to engage. Be open. Get curious. Ask questions.

In closing, I urge you to identify your perceived limitations; what beliefs are holding you back and keeping you stuck? If you think you can't – then you must. Look for signposts along the way – wisdom and opportunity come from the strangest places, often at times you would least expect.

Never stay stuck – Act! Embrace the night of the soul. If you want to discover your purpose – look for the simplicities in life. Take a step into the unknown and keep going. Your purpose will find you.

"Life is never made unbearable by circumstances, but only by lack of meaning and purpose."

~ Viktor Frankl

CHAPTER SIX

Discovering Your Purpose: Where's The Manual?

By Sandra Elston

In any one lifetime, I believe we all have an overarching purpose, and there may be several tasks to complete within that purpose.

My purpose in this lifetime is to assist the ascension of this planet and its people as strategically as possible. Within that overarching purpose is the task of destigmatizing money. Why? Because money gets a nasty rap. It is blamed for about everything. Why is that?

For instance…

If I told you that I want £500 million, would you think I'm a greedy bitch?

Would you think that £500 million is an obscene amount for anyone? Well, you're right. Of course, it is. And yet…

Money is a great tool for finding my mental blocks, and I feel it needs to be everyone's purpose to develop their wealth consciousness. My innermost money demons are practically queueing out the door to give me a hard time whenever I think about having an abundant life. I'm guessing that you may have met some of these demons too.

"You have to work hard to get money."
"Money is the root of all evil."

"You don't deserve money."
"Money corrupts."
"Money is dirty."
"Rich people are horrible."
"It's not spiritual to desire money."

I could go on. The voice in my head certainly did.

But then my brain might ask, "But is money bad?" "Is it corrupt, or does it amplify the issues already there?"

Is it unspiritual to want money? Or is rejecting money rejecting the abundance of the Universe, like a toddler throwing their lunch across the room? Now there's a thought.

I have found over time that working on my money blocks isn't just about money. It often isn't even about money at all. To name just a few, these blocks can be about:

> How I feel about myself
>
> Whether I feel I deserve good things (newsflash: I didn't!)
>
> How it negatively impacted my relationships.
>
> These blocks even impacted how I felt about my body. Amongst the many crappy beliefs, I believed, "Only rich people are slim, and rich people are nasty." How dumb is that? Some rich people are, and some aren't. They're just people with more money than me. I can tell you that that specific belief completely screwed with my diet, however. It felt like no matter what I tried, I couldn't lose weight. And why would I be able to when in my head, reaching my goal of being slim would mean that I would be nasty? What a tangled mess of beliefs that were not serving me!

It's past time these beliefs disappeared, and I will show you how. Because, in spiritual terms, money is strategically vital to living with purpose. Think about it. It's hard to focus on doing something extraordinary in the world if you don't know how to pay your gas bill. It's as simple as that.

I believe that money is a benevolent energy with wisdom all of its own. It is here to support you if you allow its presence. This is very much a matter of free will. You can decide that money is not for you. That is your choice, but are you living your purpose? If you form a partnership with money, your impact in this world can be much more. Imagine it. What could you achieve if you were fully supported by money? Dream that dream.

When I first heard that we create our reality, I looked at my life and thought, "That can't be right. My life is a disaster on legs." No way I created this. It's not what I want—nothing at all like what I want. I was working in insurance, for God's sake! No one dreams of working in insurance, and I would never discover my purpose if I stayed there!

It can be tough when you don't like your life, owning the truth you created. Really tough. Denying it and blaming someone else is so much easier, so I gave that a whirl for a while.

"None of this is my fault, you know. I'm the victim here." Naturally, this belief moved me further away from my true purpose.

It allowed me to abdicate responsibility for my life, but it didn't improve it. Instead, I was shifting the blame for everything I didn't want in my life, like working in insurance. Can you relate?

So, here's a radical idea. How about taking responsibility for my life? Hmmm. Am I sure I want to? But, of course, that would mean admitting I'm imperfect if this mess is mine. Well, that must be a bad start, surely. Or I could leave things as they are and wake up every morning knowing that I am in the wrong job living with no purpose and feeling it in every fibre of my being and dreading putting on those dull corporate clothes, picking up my briefcase and getting on the train to the city and sitting in my little grey cubicle reading contracts and writing reports that were so dull it numbed my brain. But this was my life. I had made it that way.

I had a choice. I could continue as I was, hating my life, or take responsibility for it and decide to change. This was my first step in finding my purpose. I took responsibility for my life. Examining my relationship with money came later, as you'll soon see.

To say to yourself, "Okay, this isn't the life I want, and changing it is an inside job. But I must work on myself, or my life will always be a train wreck." And a train wreck is useless to everyone, especially you, if it's your life!

I didn't know what I wanted but had definite views on what I didn't like, so I started there.

It was a bit of a no-brainer. I have created a life that I hate. One that is making me desperately unhappy, so how do I change it? The same way I made it. With my vibration. Hmmm. Say what? That's like sitting behind the wheel of a car with no idea how to drive. And everyone is doing it! And look at the results. Where's the fucking manual?

So, I started exploring the murky depths of my subconscious, looking at all these ideas about life, how to live, what I "should" be doing, what society expected of me, and about money. Could it be that some of them aren't quite right? If you don't learn to flush your toilet, you will never live purposefully.

Perhaps there is more to life than working until I'm dog-tired just so that I can pay off my mortgage?

Maybe the truth that I had drummed into me as a child: "If you work hard, you will get what you want," is wrong—even a lie designed to manipulate the working people and keep them with their noses to the grindstone.

Maybe it's okay to have money and meditate. The two don't have to be mutually exclusive.

So, I decided to open myself up to the possibility of another way of thinking. Another way of being. Another vibration.

But first, I had to get rid of the shit.

When clearing energetic blocks, I tend to *go hard or go home* to my school of thought. So, I decided that if I was going to clear my blocks, I might as well go all the way. I chose to focus on money as the tool to do that because it reliably triggers me on pretty much every subject.

This work is not for the faint-hearted. It involves looking at all those parts of your personality you wish weren't there. The sticky energy and nasty beliefs. The bits of yourself that most people never look at or call out because it's too hard. So, they have another glass of wine, switch the TV on, and pretend it's not there. That everything is fine in their life. Ignoring the ache in their soul. Choosing to numb it rather than look at it. Pretending that the pain isn't getting stronger…

But you are courageous and adventurous. You want to know why you are on this beautiful planet at this pivotal time. So let me show you how to take the first step on this path: taking responsibility for the life you are creating.

The Manual

When you partner with money, your ability to make a positive impact in the world can skyrocket, so I'm going to give the manual on how to welcome money into your life. Doing this is part of my life purpose, and I genuinely believe it will help you achieve your life purpose. It's strategic. Have a look around you. We need all the help we can get right now.

Money impacts every aspect of our lives. It is woven into every thread of our existence. It affects how we love, how we live, and how we feel about ourselves. So, what we can buy with it is just the icing on the cake.

However, this is the process of calling in whatever you want. To call in something different, you substitute it into the energetic process I teach you.

Here is a summary of the process.

Make it welcome.

- Find your blocks and do the work to dissolve them.
- Be nice to it. Take the time to get to know it and what it wants.
- Activate your wanting.
- Relax into allowing yourself to receive what you want.
- Welcome in the specific vibration of what you are calling in.
- Take the Aligned Action.
- When you receive it, care for it.

Think of your relationship with money like dating. Money has needs as well. It's not all about you! You want the world from money. You want it to love, support, and always be with you. It almost sounds like a marriage. The least you can do is make a bit of an effort too.

Does Money Feel Welcome?

To begin with, if you want money to come to you (and stay with you), you need to make it feel welcome. If you were starting a relationship and you had a choice of…

> Knocking on the grim-looking door that's firmly shut and bolted against you, or

> Strolling through a garden archway, flowers blooming and their scent drifting gently towards you. Smiling at the person who has risen to greet you and handed you a glass of wine.

Which one would you choose? Of course, I'd choose the warm welcome, but that's just me.

Money has an intelligence of its own. If it doesn't feel welcome, it won't go there. This isn't rocket science. So, look at what sort of welcome you are giving to money. Do this in whatever way works for you. Some suggestions are…

Meditation

You can meditate on this. If what you get from meditation is a bit fuzzy, you can ask for what you receive to be in a format that is easy for you to access and understand consciously. I used to get nothing but a fuzzy feeling from meditation. It is frustrating when you ask a question; knowing the answer would be very helpful! So, I request that I receive answers in a format that is easy for me to access and understand consciously. It took a while for my guides to work out the right wavelength for me so that I understood what they were sending me. It didn't happen overnight. But we persevered, and now I receive information easily.

A word of caution about meditation: I always check that whomever I connect to has been appointed by Divine Source. It's just a simple health check. Not everyone that wants to communicate with you is helpful. For this reason, I use common sense and check before I connect. Slightly off-topic but essential, nonetheless.

To meditate on this, I ask you to make contact with the welcome I am giving to money (or whatever you wish to call in). The information may come in as a feeling in my body, a picture, just a knowing.

Meditation comes in many formats, and who knew it was an amazing vehicle for unlocking your purpose? I do sit quietly on a chair and intentionally contact the Divine. This works for me. My husband goes surfing. It clears his mind. If something bothers him, he will often not return from the beach knowing the way forward. He also comes home salty and smiley, so it's all good. It's another way of accessing your inner knowing. Whatever works for you.

What is Your Intuition Telling You?

Intuition comes to us differently, and we already know our divine purpose on some level.

Something may feel right or not right.

You may know.

You may get a picture of the welcome you give money. The descriptions of the grim-looking steps above were how I first saw my welcome to money – no wonder it wasn't keen to come on in!

However, your intuition connecting with you will be unique to you. It may be one of the above or a few ways.

Your inner knowing may connect with you in another way. There is no right or wrong with this. Part of my journey has been building a relationship with my intuition by learning to recognize it. I built up trust over time, and then I began to work with it.

Check out the Vibration

You may feel the vibration of your welcome to money. How does the energy of your welcome feel?

Does the vibration feel nice? Is it high, pure, and transparent like a mountain stream? Does it bring joy to your heart? If it does, then perfect.

Alternatively, it may not be quite so lovely. If you have any money blocks, they will all show up in the vibration of your welcome to money. In all their glory! Oh, joy!

Who knew so much energetic crap could be squeezed into just one vibration? I might just run away now. It would be easier! Or I could breathe. And breathe some more because finding all my money blocks in one place could simplify everything. It has become one-stop shopping. Or one-stop releasing, to put it a better way. Just as soon as I have finished breathing into a paper bag!

So now you know what kind of welcome you are giving money. It may have been a surprise to you. It certainly was to me. I thought that I liked money. I was okay with earning a good wage and living a prosperous life. Nothing too outrageous, you understand. But comfortable. Apparently not. Those sneaky little self-sabotaging beliefs kept popping up when I wasn't looking. If you have been watching my language, you might have seen it changing in this paragraph. Contracting in, as it became something inoffensive and smaller. Something minimal. Hmm…

Release Your Blocks

It's great knowing what your money blocks. Sometimes just becoming aware of them is enough to loosen their hold on you. However, I had a lot, and their hold was more like a stranglehold around my throat, so I went for a more direct approach. Otherwise, I wouldn't ever find the keys to the toolshed to access my purpose. There are lots of tools that are great at releasing limiting beliefs. If you have a tool that works for you, that's perfect. Use it. There are so many good tools available.

The tool I have been using most recently is prayer, which I never thought I would say.

As I write this, we are halfway through the 20 years between the Cosmic moment in 2012 and the Earth's deadline to have completed its Ascension in 2032. To be blunt, the Archangel Metatron is overseeing a massive clean-up operation. We have made great strides with clearing the dense energy from the Third Dimension, but it has been much more resistant than anyone expected. Humanity has been given much help to clear the dense energy from the last 10,000 years. There is a call to awaken and live deliberately with purpose.

Normally we are told that the Light won't do our work. To a point, I think that is still correct. If someone had made no effort to clear their dense energy and then asked the angels to remove it for them and make their life wonderful with no effort, the angels may not be very impressed. However, if you have been trying to clear your energetic blocks and limiting beliefs, asking the Light for help is okay. I am skilled in energy work, and now, this tool is the one I go to daily. It is incredibly effective, and frankly, I need the help. It is a team effort. I identify what I want to be released and ask the Light to remove it for me. All you must do is ask and, of course, remember to say thank you!

Once you have released the yucky, sticky limiting beliefs, you can replace them with beliefs that create your life as you would like. But just overlaying a positive affirmation on top of them doesn't cut it, in my experience.

Be Nice to Money

And we're back to dating.

Money is not just a stack of notes or a pile of coins. Money has an intelligence and a consciousness of its own. (As do your dream job, dream relationship, and perfect business. Just substitute whatever you are working with.)

Most people have mixed feelings about money. They want to have a nice life. They want to be comfortable and taken care of. They know that money can do all of this for them. Money can provide them with ease and support them in finding their unique reason for being here. Many people don't realise we are designed to find our purpose and live meaningful lives.

But they also have limiting beliefs about money. They don't trust it, and they certainly don't love it. Most of the time, they don't even like it. So, they are sending out completely mixed messages. And then they wonder why their bank accounts have so little money.

So, take a bit of time to get to know money. After all, you invite it to spend the rest of your life with you. You ask it to love, support, and be with you always. So, putting a little time and effort into your relationship with it is the least you can do.

What does your money want? Does it like its home? Does it like what you do with it, how you use it? Is the energy of each of these clean? Or does it feel heavy and sticky to you?

The ways I do this are the same as the way I check out the vibration of the welcome I am giving money. To get to know my money (which is different from money in general) I:

Meditate with my money.

Listen to what my intuition is telling me about my money.

Check out the vibration of my money.

With each of these techniques, the aim is to. But first, listen to what *my existing* money tells me and pay attention to what it wants and needs.

Then I do the same with *what I want to call in.* I use these techniques to listen to the money I like to call in to understand its wants and needs.

When I meditated with my existing money, this is what it said to me.

> "I am sick, and I am tired. So, I move slowly like gruel.
> I want to be quick and fun and to move freely.
> To love and be loved. To be fun.
> I want to stretch my wings and fly."

I had no idea that my money felt that way. So, my job was to release the underlying beliefs causing my money to feel that way. The good news is that once you uncover your purpose as you evolve, it'll transform with you and become easier to adjust.

Activate Your Wanting

My wanting makes me nervous, to be honest. Is it safe to want? Is it safe to have? Am I even allowed a nice life? Wow. Where did that even come from?

My head knows that, yes, I am allowed to want. My job is to clear this crap and activate my wanting.

But why is wanting important? It's essential because the wanting pulls what you want toward you. It acts as a magnet. The stronger the wanting, the stronger the magnet pulling it toward you.

So, it's time to have a look at what you want. The same tools you have used before will also serve you well with this. You can meditate on your wanting. You can use your intuition to tune into your wanting. You can tune into the vibration of your wanting. And if you don't want to want anything, look at that as well. It could be another block.

To call in what you want, you need the vibration of your wanting to be high, pure, clear, and robust.

Relax and Receive

I find it very annoying being told to relax. I can feel my shoulders tensing up just thinking about it. How can anyone relax when ordered to?

But it's so important in this process of receiving. It is almost impossible to receive if you are tense, with shoulders jammed against your ears, holding yourself rigid. Nothing's going to get through that. So, you're making damn sure of it!

So, it is worth developing a practise or ritual that brings you to a state of relaxation. I take a moment to take a breath deeply. I pull the breath deep into my belly and release it gently. I keep going until I feel a deep calm and stillness. I practise it most days. (I would like to say daily, but I'm not that consistent!)

Once you feel relaxed, breathe in what you want to call in, deep into your belly, noticing how it feels.

Welcome In The Specific Vibration That You Are Calling In

I have meditated with different amounts of money. It sounds like an odd thing to do, but the vibrations of these additional amounts are all different. And they are all so delicious. It's similar to meditating with a crystal to learn its energy signature. Each crystal has its own very different energy signature. For instance, we all love rose quartz because its energy signature is the vibration of love. In that same way, different amounts of money have different energy signatures. I can get blissed out doing this!

When I meditated with £500 million, it described itself as a tsunami of love.

Who and what must I be to make that tsunami of love want to come to me?

Journal on this and let the answers flow to the page as you write.

Take the Aligned Action

You have wisdom deep within you. Now it's time to connect with that wisdom. To ask it, "What now? What do I need to do next?" This is not a mental exercise. The next step your wisdom gives you may be counterintuitive.

A friend of mine asked for clients for her new programme. Her wisdom told her to go to the supermarket and pick up some milk. While she was there, she met someone who was perfect for her programme and became a client. She could have said, "That's silly. How am I going to get a new client like that?" But she didn't. She trusted her inner wisdom and took the aligned action. So can you.

You should use common sense as well. For instance, betting every penny you have on a racehorse (or cryptocurrency) is just reckless. Your inner wisdom may push you out of your comfort zone, but it won't ask you to be reckless. If you're not sure, you can check whether it is your ego that you are tuning in to.

When You Receive It, Care For It

When you receive more money, it may not be all in one go. Chances are that it will come in little by little.

Remember, it's a relationship. You have asked for this money to come into your life. You have asked it to love, support, and make you happy. What did it ask for in return? What did you promise? What will make your money happy? What will make it want to stay with you forever?

I have applied this process to money because it triggers so much within me, and you can do so much when your money consciousness is right. Let's face it when you realise your calling will take money to pursue it. Quite literally…

And Finally…

I am here to create. To breathe life into my dreams and make them real. Flesh, blood, and bone. Able to be touched, felt, known, and savoured. Able to be loved. Able to be lived.

I am here to dance the dance of co-creation with the Universe. Breathing in the Divine Source, feeling the bliss of the connection, and letting it saturate me. I am the creator of my own experience. I created every moment and every detail in my life, and I love it. So, I have invited money to join, dance, and create with me, just for fun. Let's see where the dance takes us!

WARNING: Taking responsibility for what you believe and bring into your life carries risks. Choosing the beliefs that support the life you want to lead may cause extreme happiness, joy, and abundance. Handle with care.

You know the process now. You can choose what you make of your life. You can decide if you want money to join you and amplify your mission here. A train wreck is always an option. Or you can choose to take control of your beliefs and consciously create a purposeful life. Choose to be happy. Dare to answer the call of your soul.

It's up to you…

"The meaning of life is to find your gift. The purpose of life is to give it away."

~ Picasso

CHAPTER SEVEN

Leaving a Legacy, Finding my Purpose by Seeing the Bright Side of Life

By Jenny Bot

Dedicated to Grandma Sookey, who passed on Valentine's Day 2023, at 96 years old: August 4th, 1926 – February 14th, 2023.

I want to share some stories that have stuck with me over the years and have helped me live a purposeful life. My grandmother was a true inspiration in my life. Some memories start to fade; some still are as clear as if they happened yesterday. As I get older myself, now 41 years old, I realize what seemingly small things have impacted me profoundly, and it becomes apparent that my purpose wasn't discovered alone but with the help of many other people in my life. My grandmother was the epitome of that in my life, even more than my parents in some ways.

So let me start with the significance of our family dynamics. My grandmother was born in 1926 in Brooklyn, New York. She was the daughter of Jewish-Syrian immigrants Joseph and Freda, who came over on a steamer from Alexandria, Egypt, around 1910. She was the middle child of five in a very middle-class family. They had chickens in a tiny yard that they regularly got eggs from, and when the chickens stopped laying, they served as a nice stew. They also had boarders renting a room to earn a little extra income. The family was close, and all five were active in their local community.

My grandmother's childhood was cut short when her older brother was drafted for World War II. She was only 16 years old. She lived above a library and loved to read, but her main "job" during the war effort was to go to the top of the bell tower at their building and ring the library's air raid siren to warn the community of bombings. The war was real to her and everyone she knew; it changed her life and perspective. She lost many of her family and friends during the war. She witnessed the formation of Israel, where many of her family resettled after the war. The men came back different and changed after seeing so much loss; society was different. But people were just happy to have a chance to move on; there was so much hope.

When her brother Irving finally came home safe, she was a young adult woman who had never learned to drive; it wasn't needed where she grew up in New York. She took a leap of faith and moved in with some family that lived in California. Not long after, she met and married my grandfather.

She had three boys in the 1950s, my dad being the middle child. She loved her boys and was so proud to have raised them. She was a huge part of her community. Her community started at home with her husband and three sons, my father Joel being her second-born. I grew up going over to her house for so many family events, she was the center of gathering everyone together and planning dinners, and she was incredibly inclusive and caring toward everyone. She had a knack for looking on the bright side and had many friendships extending beyond the home. She was also close with all her neighbors and had two very close friends who lived nearby. Their kids played together growing up, and the adults formed friendships that would last a lifetime. She extended that to her Peninsula Temple Sholom, where I would learn all about Judaism. I would join the Jewish youth group, which also helped me extend my friend circle. Beyond that, she made a point to talk to people everywhere we went; it seemed like people were happy to see her. She went out every day to socialize, and she lived with purpose. Living through World War II as a teenager gave her a greater perspective of the world and how to be grateful for the little things in life, the small joys. I learned how to treat people from watching her. When I was born in 1981, I was the first granddaughter in the family. This was special to her because she had no daughters, and my whole family celebrated with me. She especially cared for me and would continue to call me every week until the end of her life.

There was one story I shared at her funeral that I would like to share with you, something I still think about every day. This single act of kindness and caring my grandmother did when I was about ten years old was instrumental to the purpose-filled life that I live today. We saw a tired-looking lady walking up a hill to a bus stop; she had just finished cleaning a house. We pulled over, and my grandmother insisted we take her home. When the lady left the car, I asked my grandmother why she had done that. She replied, "All humans suffer, but we can do something about it; we can help each other." It was that simple, but it was one of the most important moments in my life, teaching me that even if we are purpose-driven, there is still room for kindness. My grandmother was the kind of person who would light up a room. She made sure to go around and say hello to everyone, look them in the eyes, and shake their hands. When she acknowledged you, it was like you were the center of the universe for a moment. Everyone knew her name. She made a point to remember things about people and make them feel special. She truly cared, and it came from the heart. She would remember your birthday, your kids' names, and their birthdays, and she would make a point to ask you how you were. The relationships she formed because of this caring were the reward.

My grandmother gave me purpose and showed me I was worth believing in. She was there for me through so many hard times and lifted my spirit high enough that I cared for myself. I didn't discover my purpose alone. I had help from her for my entire life. I could count on her to be there for me, ensuring I got the love

I needed to grow, food, a roof over my head, and my bills paid. She made my life livable, giving me space to breathe and have time for self-care and self-discovery. I can appreciate these things because I went through dark times when I felt hopeless with no reason to live.

My family, specifically my grandmother, found me in these dark times and lifted me out every time, giving me a reason to keep going and trying. I did so, but not for myself. I wanted to make her proud and right, and I did so by doing better and learning from my mistakes. My grandmother helped me learn to forgive and let go of my anger, which was holding me back along with my fear. Despite my challenges, she always helped me focus on the bright side of things, the positives that still existed in my life. I had many opportunities ahead of me; she helped keep me focused.

The two biggest obstacles to finding my purpose were managing my anger and overcoming my fears. First, you must clear them from your path to open yourself up. Anger is a potent emotion. I was so angry in my teens; my parents getting a divorce when I was 17 seemed like the height of it. I was mad at my parents for splitting up, and I was alone from when I turned 18. I went from a 4.0 student with a bright future to failing all my classes. I was angry every day with every interaction I had. It became toxic. I always had a scowl, ready to fight anyone who accidentally bumped into me. It was a horrible feeling not being able to forgive anyone, especially myself. This feeling went on daily for years, and the anger and depression grew. It was especially important to forgive yourself and others as soon as possible to release yourself from negativity, a hard lesson for me. Without doing this, I could not focus on helping others. Finally, I realized we could choose what to focus on, the positive or the negative, in a situation. My grandmother had been showing me her whole life that both good and bad things happen; it's what we choose to focus on that gives us the power to decide if we want to be happy or not. She witnessed much human suffering throughout her life. She also believed no one should have to suffer and that we can help each other and ourselves out of that with a positive mindset, choosing to continually focus on what's going right and continue to do that. To appreciate what we have instead of focusing on what we don't. It is a choice, one you have power over. I was so angry for so long that I blinded myself to that truth. I focused on the negative; I was always so sad and angry. It became exhausting, and I got tired of it. I wanted a change. I wanted to be happy, and I understood we could either sit around and sulk and make our life worse, or we could look for the lesson and get on with things trying to do a little better every day. I choose to forgive only after years of suffering.

To keep taking steps toward my goals with her support made so many things possible in my life. My grandmother made it possible for me to attend university college. I could study biology and follow my passion for all sciences, studying physics, chemistry, biology, math, botany, and so many others.

All that extra time to follow my passions allowed me the space to find myself and my purpose. My purpose was never enough for just me, doing things for myself alone. She gave me a reason to try and instill family's importance by always being there for me. I have had many downs, making me appreciate the times of peace and health.

My grandmother was a world traveler, often bringing me back things from the countries she visited. One time, she took me on a trip when I was 19, in 2000, to New York City, where she grew up. This is significant because it was the year before the World Trade Center attack. I have a photo of us standing right in front of the buildings. I remember looking up at them, and they made my head spin. They were so tall. It was hard to believe that just one year later, they would be rubble. This trip and 9/11 shortly after had monumental effects on my life. At the time, I was in my second year of university, and my life became incredibly destabilized. I almost lost sight of my purpose.

I had a massive epiphany the moment the towers fell. It was simple. "Life is short, and you need to change anything you do not like going on right now." So, as I watched the second tower fall from my living room that morning, I took an inventory of my life and decided to make a change.

At the time, I had a boyfriend who was abusing alcohol. I was living with them when we had been dating for five years. Finally, I decided to move out on my own. There was no way I could have done this without my grandmother's support. Again, when I was making a difficult decision, she supported me. I lived alone, and for the first time in my life, I felt peace. I could decorate how I wanted to—I spent my time how I wanted to. And at 20 years old, this was a huge deal for me to be working and going to college, completely independent for the first time.

My job barely covered my bills, and my grandmother helped cover emergencies. Shortly after I moved out on my own, I was laid off from my job and given a severance package that was a considerable amount of money to me in 2002. I decided to use it all on a semester exchange program in Florence, Italy. I stayed after the semester ended to travel around the country and explore Rome and the island of Sardinia. I raked up a huge cell phone bill while there and could not pay it. Again, my grandmother covered it and bought me a plane ticket home. Her kind deed further solidified my purpose of being there for others in their hour of need, no matter how small.

When I returned to the US, I had nowhere to live. My grandmother decided she would help me by taking me around to find an apartment for the three months I needed before I moved up to a new college in the northern part of California. I had one more class I had to take before transferring in as a junior at the State School. She was determined to lay out stepping stones for me to find my purpose.

The three months I spent with her that summer significantly changed my thinking. It reinforced to me that life is short. They were in their late 70s, and they attended a funeral every week. The conversation over dinner was often about who was sick and who was dead. This was very sobering to a 21-year-old girl. Between 9/11 and the summer with my grandmother, it was a huge wake-up call not to waste time, as life is shorter than we think and sometimes comes up suddenly.

During this time, I was also experiencing remarkable social growth. I have danced since I was a kid; I took different classes at the local recreation center. I loved to dance, so I took some courses at college to learn to do ballroom or Latin dancing; I especially loved salsa dancing. When I'm dancing, the world around me doesn't exist. I feel my body, the music, and my partner's gravity. It feels like flying. I loved it so much that I went out 5-6 nights a week to dance. I didn't go to the gym; I just danced the nights away. I feel like getting in your body and out of your head it's a massive part of finding purpose in your life. It was a way to feel free and forget my worries.

And at night, when I would go home, after all the dancing, I have these incredible lucid dreams. I was also reading a lot of self-help and spiritual awareness books that got me so curious. I considered big questions about life, existence, and why we are here. I would go to sleep at night with a burning question and was waking up with the answers. There was no way for me to know without lucid dreams. Time seems to slow down in these dreams, and you can live another lifetime in one night. Where learning is limitless, and all knowledge is accessible to your subconscious mind, bridging the gap between your subconscious and conscious minds needs to be practiced. How do we make this useful? The better the question, the more helpful the answer.

But this isn't my purpose, to live to know everything. I aim to use what I learn to help people I care about. The people in my life have helped me, my family, my friends, and most importantly, my children. My path to my purpose started with my grandmother passing down all the values I learned from her example to my children. I must use what resources I must improve their lives to encourage and support their dreams. I know they will fall, but I will pick them up. I will be there when times are hard for them.

When it was about me, it was never enough to feel valued, to feel enough. I feel fulfilled when I give my purpose over to service to others. Humans aren't ever alone, although sometimes we can feel that way. It took a community to raise you, and it takes a community to raise all future generations. The more people that care and are there for others, the better our society will become. We are here to nurture each other and relieve as much suffering as possible, as the world can be a cruel place for humans.

There is a lot of loss, pain, and brutality, which is unbearable without a sense of purpose or reason to live with love, warmth, and light.

What is your inner voice? When someone says you can do it, you think, "I can do it too!" You can also be that voice for someone else, continuing the cycle of encouraging each other. Ultimately, the point is that we need others to help us find our purpose and help others. Every person can be a part of this community, a network of humans helping humans. Your purpose isn't to do something for yourself but for others.

My daughter, named after my grandmother, has become my purpose. Now I carry on our family's legacy so that future generations will benefit from all our collective experience. Repeating the things I have learned to help her, she has also given back to my joy from just being together. I am watching her grow up and learn new things. She is now ten years old and is becoming a beautiful young lady. When we attended my grandmother's funeral last month, we had a nice service with all our family. I think my grandmother would have been proud to see all her children, grandchildren, and great-grandchildren sharing memories and celebrating her life.

I want to be a cheerleader for good. I want to encourage others to try every day to do their best. I want to enable humans to care for themselves and forgive themselves and others. I want to be a part of creating communities of people that support each other. My purpose is so much bigger than just myself. I want to champion being an advocate for yourself and being an advocate for others. There is no greater feeling than truly wanting to make the world a better place, not by some grand event, but by every small gesture you can. All those little things add up to something much greater—a sense of purpose, belonging, and well-being.

I volunteer at my daughter's school and make time to be active in their lives. This is an essential thing that gives me purpose in my life. Most of my energy goes toward future planning, family events, and outings. And I would say my life now is very fulfilling. I am happier than I have ever been before. I plan to plant a new garden soon; I love watching the plants grow. Even a study says gardening helps people with anxiety, something I didn't know, but it makes sense. Being out in nature and calm makes it easier to feel like you are part of something greater. Looking up at the night sky, and seeing all the other places in the universe, can make you feel tiny, but knowing you can impact other people's lives can make you feel incredibly large. For a long time, I thought my purpose was to invent great scientific discoveries. I realize that might happen now, but it's not nearly as important as my actions and relationships with others. There is a cumulative effect to a life full of good deeds versus a life of apathy or anger.

Teaching others has become the next progression. I've been starting online communities, bringing people together who might not feel part of something. There are many ways to do this, but what's important is that you start joining communities you are interested in and start somewhere. If you don't vibe with it, keep trying new things until you find something that makes you feel at home. Life is an adventure; it's as interesting as you make it. Helping others is the biggest gift we have. It's the spiritual gift that keeps on giving to your soul itself. It is our true purpose. Since none of us are alone here, we all need help as much as we need to give it to others.

You can wander through life aimlessly without purpose. Or purpose can find you. But I have discovered many helpful ways of getting me into the right mindset to gain clarity.

The most important thing is not how old you are when you read this but that you are ready to fully commit to being your best person. Are you ready to follow through and gain more trust in yourself? There will always be obstacles and excuses, but when you decide you want something, you must stick to it to attain your goals. To start, you need a clear vision of your "why?" Why are you reading this book? What part of your life do you want to see changes in? What are the questions you haven't asked yourself yet or are afraid to ask?

When we practice mindfulness, we can fully enjoy our moment without anxiety about the future or thoughts of the past. So, I ask you to commit to the journey that awaits you. Fear often holds us back; it did for me for many years. Fear is overthinking things that haven't happened yet, so let's begin now. Look around at our surroundings, take in all the senses, sights, smells, and noises around us, and notice how different things make us feel. Do you have anything in your life you feel excited about when you wake up in the morning? Passion leads to purpose. You must find joy in your daily life. So, keep your playfulness present; even in times of grief or doubt, we must carve out moments of joy for ourselves. Trust and respect yourself. Forgive yourself, don't hold grudges against others.

For me, finding a passion for things has always come easily. This is probably because of my obsessiveness. I get into something when I start learning new information about something that excites me; I can almost get lost; I get so focused on learning as much as possible. But passion is not the same as purpose, which certainly leads to it. It has come full circle for me, where I fill up my cup so much it overflows into others. Other people, other areas, and the world as we know it. There is this intricate balance for self-awareness and care, empathy for others, and interconnectedness, and we must balance both.

Affirmations have been a huge part of my personal growth. Being mindful of our inner dialog directly affects our outer world. It takes time and commitment before you can change your habits biologically. However, if you commit to at least seven days for each new idea and 30 days for each action, you can reprogram yourself with better habits. Remember, the key is moderation; giving yourself time to reflect on the ideas you're learning and integrate them doesn't happen overnight. It's going to be over weeks, months, and years that you see lasting change.

We often forget that the first part of changing is wanting to change. You have already taken action to show you are ready, open, and willing to be who you are truly meant to be. Write I LOVE YOU on a piece of paper and tape it to your mirror every morning; say it to yourself, look yourself in the eye, and mean it. Also, write ten things you feel like you are good at and tape them to the mirror. Remind yourself of your whys; "why am I doing this?" It's important to reflect and ask yourself questions that lead to the answer you need to progress your mind and life.

That internal conversation you have with yourself is the first step to healing. What are your thoughts, what are you telling yourself, and how do you feel about yourself? These are the things we often sit and think about ourselves, but we often need to start doing healthy things for ourselves. Take a walk, bath, exercise, whatever gets you up and moving. Getting stuck in our devices, TV, Computer, and Cell phones are so easy. We need time away from those things daily to stretch, relax, decompress, and reflect. You must try things until you find something that works for you. Mastering yourself is the path to finding and living your purpose.

As a mother of three, I know how busy it can get, you get caught up sometimes taking care of everyone else and putting yourself at the end of the day, but I will tell you right now that won't work out well in the long run. You must be an example of how to treat yourself; modeling this behavior will benefit everyone in your family. I invite you to write down lists of what you want to accomplish today, this month, and this year and use them as a rough guide to your daily priorities. To keep yourself focused, keep this list somewhere you look every day. Make sure you have specific goals that are actionably helping evolve your purpose.

You must release all pain from the past to give yourself the love you need to feel worthy of having a purpose. Self-love is universal love; we are all a part of the universal mind. You can raise other moods, too, by staying in your bliss. Your purpose will come to you like a passion; you will wake up thinking about it first thing in the morning. If you aren't there yet, you must discover what to do. You are now on a mission to find that information waiting for you.

Think of life like an action-adventure movie you're starring in. You are roleplaying whom you want to become by acting like them. The intent to seek it out begins taking you toward true self-discovery. Fear will isolate you and hold you back from learning truths that you may see as scary, but let me tell you, the thing you should fear is fear itself.

We learn many things that won't inspire us, but when you find something that makes your soul sing, it will be like a lightning bolt up your spine, energizing you to act. Consider this: what made you buy and read this book in the first place? What catalyst in your life led you right here to read these words? And for that, you have taken the first step to open yourself up to a different perspective you may not have thought of. We are a collective society of eight billion collaborating minds.

Once you have let go of all fear by diving into and through them, a huge weight will be lifted from your spirit, and your true path will reveal itself to you. Furthermore, just by telling others of your intent, you will start attracting people who can help you. Don't forget; we can't make this journey alone. And the people you need to surround yourself with should also be open-minded. If you tell these ideas to close-minded people, they will shut you down because of their fears. Therefore, it's imperative to keep negativity about yourself away from your inner self. Instead, commit yourself to maintaining a positive outlook.

You can take control of what you see, keeping your intent in mind to find your purpose, and mute or unfollow anyone who is taking away from your peace, joy, or progress. Then add topics, groups, hobbies, affirmations, and photography of things you enjoy looking at in abundance. You will notice this will immediately affect your mood for the better. Remember, you are attracting what you put into the universe, speaking and writing what you want to happen into existence. One positive word can make someone's day, and one negative can ruin it. So, use your power of words wisely to attract your purpose.

You can decide to reinvent yourself at any time. You don't have to feel stuck where you are, in your mind or body, if you choose to shift. You have choices: staying where you are or moving in a certain direction. No matter how hard we hold onto what we feel we are now, five or ten years from now, we will be different people because of our experiences, so why not take ownership of that direction to become the person you want to be? It starts with a vision, and then the path reveals itself slowly. Begin walking in that direction one step at a time and permit yourself to start.

"When you walk in purpose, you collide with destiny."

~ Ralph Buchana

CHAPTER EIGHT

Heal Your Story to Find Your Life Purpose

By Maria Jesus Campos

PROUD OF WHOM I HAVE BECOME

Who am I? This was a question that took me years to clarify. Honestly, I wasn't doing much to get clarity, and it felt that I had different purposes in different seasons of my Life. But deep inside, I knew something bigger was waiting for me.

I have worked to find my purpose and reached the best moments in my life through this journey. I have created my health, recovered from everything I was carrying, and released my internal pain. I am a much better version of myself than I used to be, and at 40 years old, I created with my kids the life I truly wanted to live in.

I now completely trust my body and the universe, which wants nothing else but to support me.

So, I live beyond my dreams and am open and ready to move further.

But it wasn't always like this. It was quite a journey coming to this point.

BECAUSE OF WHO I WAS

I always worked to improve, learn, and progress when I was young. Yet, I had the feeling it was never enough to fill in the expectations of others, to feel more loved, and to feel recognized. Nobody told me that being myself was enough, so I constantly battled between being excellent and the guilt of not reaching that aim.

Why did I need to be perfect? Because I was looking to be loved, seen, and heard. I had to accomplish what others wanted from me or my version of what they expected. Little did I know how important this was to find my true purpose.

What is perfection?

The answer to this question surely depends on the level of self-love that each of us has. More self-love means more self-acceptance, compassion, and understanding of who we are. Consequently, the importance of perfection disappears.

Since becoming a mom, I have understood real love with compassion and honesty, no judgment, no barriers, and no "buts." The beauty of this process wasn't just the existence of my two kids but this new feeling coming out of my own heart toward my children. One day, I could feel this for myself as well.

Like many of you, I always tried to help and be there for others, mostly satisfying the needs of others before meeting my own needs. I aimed to try to be better for others, fitting in the society and the norm.

I was never normal, even though I tried hard to be, which was exactly what killed my true version.

Trying to adapt to what I believed was normal brought me consequences that changed my health forever.

Losing my dad and being unhappy in my marriage, which I couldn't make "perfect" as I thought it should be, brought chaos inside of me.

I carried much pain from my past. Being unable to speak up about my problems and neglecting my emotions resulted in a numb and sick body.

I was a sad mom. I was angry. I used to put guilt into others. Consequently, I developed an autoimmune disease.

At 27, I transformed from a sporty girl to trapped in a 100-year-old body with constant bone and muscle pain. Every day the sensation was like having a fever, being weak, and sincerely depressed. I had no energy and wanted to stay in bed, but my mind was telling me to go, not to listen to my body crying for help: "I cannot do it anymore; I am done!"

How do you learn to live in constant physical and emotional pain? I learned to carry it silently with the Sjogren Autoimmune Disease, chronic fatigue, fibromyalgia, chronic anemia, ulcers, and rheumatoid arthritis. Suppressing the sadness and anger of being sick was the only thing I knew how to do.

All the sports I used to do, I couldn't anymore. I was dropping everything because my hands had no strength and were in pain. It was even painful to hold my baby in my arms. Anything that gave me a sense of purpose was a challenge. People thought I was clumsy because I didn't say much about what was happening to me. And the ones that knew sometimes doubted. I was told, "You don't feel ache; you are just depressed; it is all in your head," like I was inventing it all. But for me, it felt very real. Little did I know that it would lead me to uncover my purpose.

Becoming a mother was risky, but it saved my life!

My first child was born with severe allergies, and we were terrified of losing him. I suppressed the reality of my agony once more; I took all the necessary medication and decided to stay focused on my son. I needed to use all my strength and hope to save my baby this time. At the worst moment, we had no choice but to admit him to the hospital for an unknown time.

My instinct was shouting that we had to do something else. I was afraid of hospitals after losing my dad. I prayed, and the solution came through a friend. My heart firmly guided me to take risks and cross borders to find a solution. We flew to Costa Rica from Chile to see Dr. Kim Ok Gwan, someone my friend recommended. My baby started to heal immediately, opening a door of hope for me. Maybe I could also heal. He cleansed us both through special acupuncture and food. We discovered nutrition, healing, and a future with new possibilities.

Slowly with time, my body started detoxing, changing, and healing. My good days were more than the bad days, and my mood changed because the soreness was less and less every day. I finally felt hope that I had a solution and could live longer to be there for my kids. So, I decided to take the chance to fight my destiny.

Until that moment, I had learned all I could about nutrition. For ten years, I experimented with many different therapies, which on the journey, taught me how to heal my body. I had healed 70% of it with nutrition, but the other 30% was still ghosting me, and finding it became my new purpose.

When we moved to Switzerland, I felt that it was an opportunity. I had no entertainment around, no judgment or distractions from others. For the same reason, the emotional agony became very raw. Every time my body brought me down, I took the time to restart it, but I was always afraid of what could happen in the future because I couldn't do everything as before. I became scared of and fully dependent on my body; I was afraid to die. I thought that if I was born healthy, and it was me who triggered the sickness, the solution should also be in me.

In 2017, I had an awakening in which I understood that happiness was a choice, not something that comes because of doing or having. That "moment" was when I declared to the universe, "I choose to be happy because it is good for my health." I had the right and the obligation to be happy! This was my new purpose, to discover my inner happiness.

After that, many doors opened, and I received all the help I needed from coaches and healers. They taught me to stop looking to heal on the outside and to start healing from the inside. It was then that the miracles started happening. I had reconstructed myself as I wanted. Finally, I could decide who I wanted to be and how I wanted to feel inside and out.

I had to release the emotional suffering that weakened my immune system. After that, my bone pain was gone, and my labs came back completely clean. It was hard to believe, especially for my doctors. I started collecting data at that moment because this was bigger than I could imagine.

From my coaches and both of my incredible kids, I have learned what real love is; how to open to accept healing and to expand in ways that I didn't think were possible. Being a single mom in a foreign country brought me one breakthrough after another. From moments of stress and desperation, thinking that I could not do it, to realizing that I could expand once and again. From thinking that I had to do it because my kids were counting on me to believing I deserved to be better for myself.

My children have inspired me to work on myself, to be the woman, mother, and human I always wanted to be for them and me.

Now, healthier than ever, with all my energy, I am passionate about loving, living, and developing my true purpose.

I want to leave a blueprint on this planet. So, I help awaken people that say "yes" to bio-hack their true best self, health, and wealth by healing their body, mind, and spirit. Through nutrition, mindset, and conscious movement, I teach them to connect with the true source of love and release their past and suffering. Moreover, I show them how to find balance, clarity, and the courage to reclaim their right to be happy and healthy.

It took me 11 years to get my health back. I thank the journey which showed me I was proof that you can heal yourself. Would you want to be the proof too?

Imagine the past doesn't own you. Imagine yourself in your dream body, recovering your focus and memory, feeling your brain as never before. You can live lighter and move faster to the future you would love to be in. You can take your body where you need to, and the mind will follow.

How would you prepare your body to receive the abundance you want?

EVIDENCE

Having come from a Business and Economics career, as expected, my purpose was working and raising money to have the life I wanted. It sounds reasonable, but I completely disconnected from myself, not knowing who I was and pushing myself into a model I had created.

This purpose had no content or roots; it was about pushing forward, not allowing myself to rest. Resting made me feel useless, but my body and health didn't come with that plan.

Thank God, my first child came to reeducate my family and me about our nutrition so we could better understand the importance of what we ate.

Focus on your body and live through "You are what you eat." "Knowing how to use good food can completely change your health, mood, and feelings."

When you live in an unhappy cycle, it is hard to break out of it. Food was my starting point. In the past, I had eaten food bad for me, so I had to use good food to reverse my condition.

After a few years of changing my diet, I still looked for that 30% of health I was missing.

I was considered weird because when we moved to Switzerland, doctors didn't know my story; they didn't even believe it. With all the exams as evidence, they couldn't understand how I felt so good without taking corticoids. When I decided to be happy because it was good for my health, I commanded health and happiness in my body, and the healing process accelerated.

My mom told me once she had observed that I felt better whenever my husband traveled. That opened my eyes! So, containing my sentiments made me feel sick. There was something! Emotions and trauma directly influenced my immune system. So, I started observing. When my last crash happened, it was connected to a bad experience during the holidays, where I ended up in a hospital between a perforated intestine diagnosis and hepatitis. That was the proof I was looking for.

From then on, I decided to add to my ever-refining purpose, healing my traumas and understanding how they affected my spirit and body. I separated from my husband and started working on my past traumas, self-love, and confidence. This led to my ability to speak up, listen to my body, love myself, see who I was, and connect all my fragmented pieces. Separation is not a cure, but in my case, I needed to be alone to heal. My body became lighter, and I had no pain in my neck, joints, or muscles. My voice grew stronger, and I started awakening from my numbness. I could see myself with compassion, stopped the judgment, witnessed things from a brighter reality, and completely buried the victim I was. I still didn't know my true-life purpose exactly, but I knew I was moving in the right direction without thinking about it.

Looking back, I could have been faster in my healing process, but it took me too long to ask for help. I used to focus much more on the daily problems than the ones in me.

We come to the world to depend on our parents for a while. Part of becoming an adult is detaching from their parents and becoming responsible for their needs and life. We know this, but we often don't act as we know. We keep complaining about what we were missing in the past and whose fault it was.

After my dad died, I was angry with him because he chose not to fight back against cancer. The neediness can come from childhood trauma, even without any deficiency of love. Losing my dad and my separation pushed me to take complete responsibility for my life and accept that no one was to blame. I have taken charge of my happiness and have embraced the freedom to choose!

"Don't pass the responsibility of being happy and loved to others because you will be dependent. Only you know better what you need and how you want it. Being a responsible adult will empower you forever."

Just because I said Yes to me, many doors started to open. I was offered help, and I jumped to take it. It was my first self-love journey. I was used to the fact that it was ok to invest in my career and studies, but never in me, in my spirit. I could spend money on millions of doctors, gyms, and things that were "normal." But coaching was something new for me. It was the answer to my prayers because, since the first time I was there, I knew I had found my missing piece.

My soul started evolving and healing quickly, and I could finally be vulnerable when needed. I connected healing paths with people who gave me love and protection without any expectations. That is why I called it home! Have you ever felt this? When you feel that you belong, you finally find and connect with yourself and feel complete, even if you still have traumas or pain. It sounds like paradise; believe me, it feels like it too.

"The importance of going inside to find a home within us, with no roles to play, no emotions to suppress, only being, is essential to find a safe space to be who you truly are. Acceptance and love for yourself are a big start."

My coach, Mahima Klinge, showed me how to love, recognize and accept myself as I was, getting in touch with "the" pure love. Finally, I found the source of the love I unconditionally gave my kids. This time, I connected with it and opened the lid to make it constantly flow toward me.

Lisa Nichols showed me that as a single mom, I could feel complete and that having it all was possible.

Slowly the real Maria started shining out, my intuition became clearer, and I was ready to look for my true-life purpose.

"We don't need to invent how to do it; it becomes faster when you askfor the correct help from someone that has already done it."

My coach, Gisela Rocha, taught me that healing our spirits, traumas, and sicknesses was possible. With Movement for Life, I have healed traumas and beliefs I wasn't even aware of.

Healing from my past, my negative and judgmental thinking, and the negative people and environments, gave space to my body to be filled with love and to heal by itself.

"Emotions will come either way; you cannot control them, but what you can do, is to control what you do with them. With movement medicine, your emotions will naturally flow through and out of your body and their healing-releasing process will go where your mind will not interfere."

Layer after layer of judgment, lack of self-love, extra weight, bad immune system, and other pains showed the size of my disconnection. I didn't erase my story but stopped living from the pieces that constructed it. I healed those pieces and made them part of my discovery journey. That is what makes me the woman I am today.

Trauma is not what happens to you but what happens inside you. Trauma is a disconnection from ourselves, and health is the reconnection. The capacity of healing is simply in our natural organism, so all we must do to heal is reconnect.

What if everyone's purpose was to heal their traumas?

It took me 11 years of investigation to connect all I have learned to feel secure enough to share it. "Nobody should be condemned to a diagnosis; everybody should enjoy the best of their brain and body." I thought my fate was written after the doctor's diagnosis. My future seemed much shorter than expected, and medication would be the only way to survive.

This was big; I changed my fate! All that life brought me was a series of connections and the correct help to show me the path to finally say: that I am 100% healed and ready to share my purpose with passion. In 2018 I was healed forever!

I cured myself for a reason. The door of sickness was finally closed, and the door of health was wide open with opportunities and a new purpose in my life. The purpose of healing my body was accomplished, and the purpose of healing my emotional pain was covered and in progress so I could focus on discovering who I was. I took one step at a time, and it was then that I got the structure from my coaches to ask myself whom I wanted to be and how I wanted to feel. I started dreaming freely again because I was certain I would have a future by then.

I carry a phrase: "If your dreams don't scare you, it is because you are not dreaming enough." I promised myself that I could have it all. Not all at once, but step by step. I often repeated the exercise of thinking, what I wanted to be for the rest of my life? What was my uniqueness? As I always share, the work I have done is not only mine but also from the universe. It has also been a partnership and dance among all the people that have crossed my journey, and to them, I say: "Thank you."

Working with nutrition, mindset, movement, and various techniques taught me how to connect the body, mind, and spirit to help myself and others. I understood that my business career and being a mom weren't the true purposes of my life; they were just the steps to it. Discovering my source of true love brought me healing and health, and with that came real abundance.

"Let yourself accept where you are right now with compassion, and from there, help yourself to open your body and mind for abundance. Allow yourself to dream, ask for help, and the 'how' will come."

In 2019, my instinct was telling me to be a Coach. It felt good; it felt reasonable. But how could I shift my career from Business to Coaching? I knew my past wasn't just a coincidence.

After I said Yes to being a Coach and sharing my healing process, I had no idea how to do it.

The "how" is the least important! Afterward, during the Covid pandemic, I started connecting and making weekly calls with old friends when my university friends told me to coach them. Boom! The opportunity was in front of me. I doubted, and I was scared. Nevertheless, I said yes.

My friends had no idea what they were getting into. I took it seriously, like "the opportunity of my life." How often can you practice something before knowing if you want to work on it without risk? Truly, always!

I am a bit of a nerd, so I structured it very quickly. I built a one-year program to work on their SELF, HEALTH, and WEALTH. After a long year and having vibrated in every class I did for my first clients, I told the universe: "This is it! It's my purpose, I could do this daily, even for free."

Finally, I jumped out of bed happy, ready to do more. I felt it in my bones but didn't know how to put it out there. But I trusted this was it, and Wioletta Simonet came to support me step by step while building my business.

When you build your business, many things will stretch you as never before, so you must be doing what makes you vibrate very high. If not, it will not last. In the bad moments, I repeatedly asked myself: could I do this daily? And the answer has always been yes for me since 2019.

IN PURSUIT OF YOUR PURPOSE

DON'T ...	DO...
1. ignore or carry the weight of your story and your body's physical or emotional pain.	1. heal your story and use it to create your future. Forgetting or overcoming is not healing. Do the work! You can be scared to open Pandora's box and confront your emotions, but guess what? You will be living in Pandora's box forever if you don't do it.
2. do it all by yourself. It will always feel like it is a lot.	2. ask for help if you haven't done it yet. Don't wait anymore. You don't need to discover anything new. To do it faster, follow the steps of someone that has already done it.
3. expect that your purpose will come to you like magic. Maybe wait forever.	3. be open to receiving mentors that know how to do it. Finding the purpose is easier than you imagine, but it needs work and focus.
4. ever sat down to dream about your future version? Instead, wait for later, for the perfect moment. Never have time or think it is impossible.	4. sit down to dream and think where, with whom, and how you want to feel in the future. In your body, your career, relationships, finances, and your surroundings. "If your dreams don't scare you, you are not dreaming enough."
5. keep focusing on what you don't do well. This brings judgment, and it slows you down.	5. focus on what you do well and what you do best. Identify and develop your strengths. You will succeed faster than you imagine.
6. forget your values or be confused about them.	6. be clear about the core values for which you will stand up.
7. never stop asking yourself important questions.	7. Once and again, answer these important questions, and put all your ideas together: What do I love doing? What do I do well? In what ways can I serve the world? What do I love doing? HOBBY CHARITY THE ANSWER What do I do well? PROFESSION JOB In what ways can I serve the world?

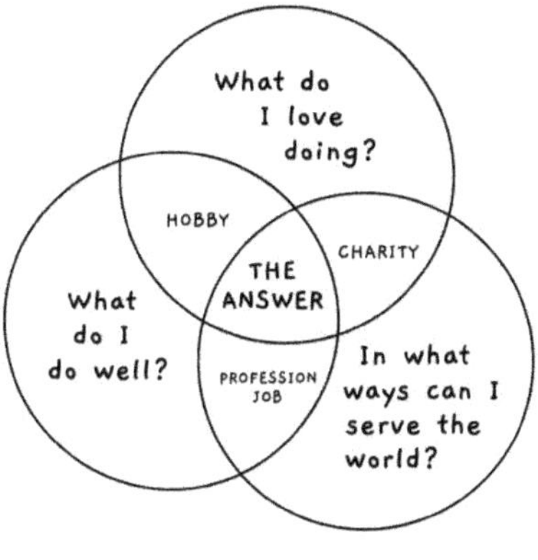

8. do it only if you know you will be successful and earn much money. 9. center your work depending on the consistency of your motivation. 10. limit yourself to starting something just because the perfect moment never comes. There are a million excuses that will keep on coming. Being ready is overrated. 11. stop trying because of the fear of failure or freeze whenever you are afraid to do something new. 12. lack consistency even if you get uncomfortable. 13. try to do a million things at the same time. 14. leave aside your basic human needs and yourself in general. Don´t push your body to its limit. Giving constantly to others without putting yourself first will take you to emptiness and burnout.	8. do it even for free till the last day you are alive. The purpose is a reason to live; it shouldn't feel like work. 9. remember that motivation comes and goes. Even in the worst moments, inspiration will come again if you practice your passion. Purpose is passion. 10. start now! Don't wait to be ready. You might never be prepared, and life could pass you by. 11. try small! Take small steps so there is no big risk and no fear that will paralyze you, but do it EVERY DAY! Trial and error—practice before jumping higher. 12. do something NEW every day, like a mental gym, to stretch your mind and get used to being uncomfortable. 13. focus on one thing at a time. Learn to prioritize; it is a golden rule. Ask yourself often, "What is an urgent matter?" Select three and then order them by life importance. 14. satisfy your basic human needs daily before even thinking about giving to others. To provide a better quality of what you give, you must first fulfill your needs with nothing else but the best.

The visualization of your dreams depends directly on your healing. How we see the world relates to our old beliefs and story. What happens every time we heal part of our story is that our mind, body, and patterns change, and we can transcend our reality. We see further, more positively, and more abundantly.

If you want abundance to become a reality, work on yourself, heal your story, and your brain and body will follow with health forever, to live and share the joy of your purpose.

"If you can tune into your purpose and really align with it, setting goals so that your vision is an expression of that purpose, then life flows much more easily."

~ Jack Canfield

CHAPTER NINE

I Found My Purpose, Hidden in My Greatest Life Challenge

By Nerida Winters

Do you ever wonder why you are here on this earth right now? Do you ever wonder what difference you can make in this world? Do you ever wonder what your purpose is? Do you ever wonder if something way bigger than you is going on? Perhaps you're just a puzzle piece in this game we call life. Maybe you must find other puzzle pieces and fit them together to find the answers to these questions.

I have to say I don't think I ever thought to ask myself any of those questions until recently in my life. My life was simply one of existence. Don't get me wrong: I have had a great life, but it has been mostly filled with doing. I've rarely had a spare moment in my day that I didn't fill up with something. Working full-time, raising children, training, and competing with dogs and horses – I didn't stop. I saw life through a lens of what I thought was expected of me. Grow up, get married, have children, work hard, retire, and die happy. That has always been viewed as the standard of success in the circles that I have lived in.

I think I did so many things to drown out a feeling of something missing. Secretly, I was seeking more. I was seeking something I didn't even know or understand. I was pursuing my purpose, my purpose for living, my reason for existing on earth.

I don't think I had even contemplated the meaning of having a purpose until I was in my forties. This was when the universe took over and put me into some situations that made me ask questions and change how I viewed my place in the world.

My name is Nerida Winters, and this is my story about how I discovered my purpose.

On the 30th of May 2014, I sat in the doctor's office, taking in everything she said to me. "You have breast cancer! It is a reasonably large lump, but from the biopsy, it's only stage 2." She referred me to a surgeon to determine my treatment. "I don't think I've ever had somebody take this news as calmly as you have," she said. It was indeed a lot to take in, but in my soul, I already knew that I had cancer and that this was just a process I needed to go through to find health again. Little did I know that this event would set me on my way to discovering my purpose.

At no point did I ever feel that my life was at risk, but telling my family was the hardest thing I ever had to do? Even as I write this now, tears are streaming down my face. Of course, it is hard for a mother to tell her children that she has cancer and her life is at risk, but I knew it would hit them extra hard. Only three years earlier, they had lost their dearly loved grandmother to pancreatic cancer.

At first, I thought I would only need a lumpectomy and radiation treatment and could return to work within a couple of weeks. However, when my results returned after my surgery, I was told they didn't get it all and that it was also in three of my lymph nodes, and I needed to return to the hospital the following week for a mastectomy. That hit me hard because I had been so clear in my mind. Perhaps I was trying to control the situation, imagining that I would be through this quickly and easily and continue with my life. The universe had other ideas, and now I was recommended to have another painful surgery followed by additional chemotherapy and radiation treatment.

"We can't control everything that happens to us, but we can control how we respond to things we can't control."

- Avis J. Williams

It's funny – as I write this, I realize that if I hadn't been genuinely stopped in my tracks to go through all the treatment I did and to experience being at home and focusing on myself, I probably would not have discovered my purpose. So, it was indeed a blessing that one year before my diagnosis, my husband at the time and I had purchased the most beautiful property just outside Bungendore, New South Wales, Australia. There was no better place to be for my recovery.

"In the presence of nature, a wild delight runs the man, despite real sorrow."
– Ralph Waldo Emerson

On the morning of my first chemotherapy treatment, one of our steers was missing from the paddock, but we didn't have time to search for him as my appointment was early, and the drive to the hospital took nearly an hour. So, as we went home after my treatment, I asked my husband to drop me off at the entrance to the creek that ran through our property as I walked to see if I could locate the steer. It was important to find him as he would have access to the highway, which was dangerous to him and any vehicles traveling by.

It was around 11:00 am, and although it was winter, it was a clear and sunny day. It was quite warm for that time of year. I saw the steer quickly and started walking him back along the creek to our property. It took me two hours to get him home. Two beautiful, glorious hours of strolling along the stream under the trees, listening to the water and the birds, and observing wildlife. It was just him and me. That walk was one of the most healing experiences that will be etched in my mind forever. That afternoon I slept right through to the next morning and woke up ready to take on the day. I believe this time in nature helped me move quickly through this first round of treatment. Rather than search for my purpose, I found that moments of reflection connected with nature enabled me to understand myself on a deeper level, allowing my purpose to find me.

Animals are one of my greatest loves. I love all animals but am most passionate about my horses and dogs.

We had around six horses at the time. They needed to be fed and cared for twice a day. My treatment was physically demanding, so I was very grateful for the help and support of my family during this time. I always ensured that I went outside to help with the chores regardless of how I felt. Being out in nature with the horses always made me feel whole and well again. Honestly, there is nothing like getting rid of a headache or waking you up when feeling tired than spending a little time outside in nature. I was blessed that throughout my whole treatment journey, there were only a few days when I was too unwell to go outside.

I continued to ride and train the horses at a more sedate pace than I would typically have been. I realize now that going slowly and steadily is the most effective way to train animals and to be in life. When you take the time to get a solid foundation and allow yourself the time to think deeply and understand the basics, everything else comes more easily and quickly. I knew that working with horses was my passion and part of my purpose, but strangely I didn't realize the puzzle pieces that would make it financially viable.

"When educating horses, there is no greater maxim then slow is fast and fast is slow."
- Monty Roberts

Throughout my seven months of treatment, I rode, took my daughter to competitions, competed, trained a horse, and participated in clinics. I never really saw myself as "sick." Best of all, I got to take time and hang out with the horses. Perhaps for the first time in my adult life, I had time to be and get to know the horses more deeply. To start to understand and connect with them and with myself.

On one glorious summer's day toward the end of my chemotherapy treatment, I was lying on the banana lounge under a tree, watching my daughter ride our horse, Elvis. She is a kind, thoughtful and beautiful rider, and I love watching her ride. I reflected on how wonderful I felt at that moment. It was a lovely place to be, happy, calm and peaceful. I reflected on my journey and realized how easy it had been overall. But then, I felt a huge rush of love and excitement as it truly hit me that I wanted to share this experience with others. To support others on their life journey, to help others heal through horses, animals, and nature, just like I did. To assist others in finding an easier journey in their life.

"Your work will fill a large gap in your life, and the only way to be truly satisfied is to do what you believe is great work. And the only way to do great work is to love what you do. So if you haven't found it yet, keep looking. Don't settle. As with all matters of the heart, you will know when you find it. And, like any great relationship, it just gets better and better as the years roll on. So keep looking until you find it. Don't settle.

- Steve Jobs

I had always wanted to work with animals. I enrolled in Agricultural College when I left school, but my mum's mental health issues meant I needed to stay home and help care for her. So, I applied for a vet nurse job in our local town. Unfortunately, the vet sat me down and told me it was a dead-end job. He told me to go into the world and get a real job. So, I enrolled at the local TAFE for a year and completed Secretarial Studies before heading to the nearest city, Canberra, to work in the public service.

Nonetheless, I have always trained and cared for animals personally and voluntarily over the years. I became a dog obedience instructor and was involved in Flyball. I have rescued and rehomed around 200 dogs over my lifetime—a challenging but gratifying thing to do. We have also saved a few horses. At pony club with my daughter, I became an instructor to help and support the kids to be their best for their horses. I don't do as much now as my job, farm, and working toward my purpose takes all my time.

There are so many things I always wanted to do with the animals full-time, but the thing that always came up was that it would not make enough money. As I was the primary breadwinner in the family, I couldn't risk not making enough income for our family, so those ideas were always put on the back burner. However, I yearned deep in my soul to do something to serve the animals.

When I am working with people and animals, the hours disappear. I get so much joy from seeing the people and animals grow together and the smiles on people's faces. My daughter, who has excellent boundaries, always pulls me up and reminds me to stick to the schedule. I am still establishing my boundaries all these years on. I discovered that when I do what I love, time doesn't exist, and as they say, when we love what we do, we don't work a day in our life. I realize now that we love doing something so much because it is why we are here. We are here to share the love. To love what we do and to share that love and passion with others. This is where we truly start to discover our purpose in life.

"If you can't figure out your purpose, figure out your passion. For your passion will lead you right into your purpose."
- Bishop T.D. Jakes

In 2016 I decided to take steps to follow my purpose and create a business to help others through horses. The first step was to develop the skills and obtain the necessary qualifications. My daughter joined me as a business partner, and we pursued obtaining our qualifications together. Unfortunately, it was going to cost quite a bit of money to get the necessary qualifications.

I learned to say "yes" to things. Throughout my life, we have always lived from paycheque to paycheque. As young children, we often could not even afford electricity. With this background, I found spending money with my money mindset hard. I always kept myself small by not stepping into opportunities.

Our first qualification was in rider biomechanics with Colleen Kelly. We passed our theory tests, but to complete our Rider

Biomechanics qualifications, we would need to travel to Kentucky in the United States of America to undertake the practical test. For the first time, I said "yes" to myself. I wasn't sure how I would pay for everything, but we decided my daughter, sister, and I would all go. Although this was my first experience traveling overseas, my sister is a seasoned traveler and came to chaperone us and help us enjoy our first overseas trip together. Amazingly, we were gifted money for the airfares and accommodation. This was a wonderful blessing. All we needed was a little spending money.

After much work on my personal growth, I now understand that when you open yourself to opportunities, say "yes," and work towards them, what will come to you. Aligning with one's purpose creates synchronicities that bring the puzzle pieces together.

"Gratitude is a powerful process for shifting your energy and bringing more of what you want into your life. Be grateful for what you already have, and you will attract more good things."

- Rhonda Byrne

In 2017, we opened our business, Lyndonlea Equine. Our main service involved taking our miniature horses into nursing homes and hospitals. To watch people who didn't talk, talk, those who struggled to walk, walk and those who were in deep depression smile and laugh – the feeling is indescribable. Working with patients, residents, and staff brought me so much joy. Later in 2017, Ellen and I obtained our qualifications in Equine Assisted Learning to build on our business of helping others.

I wanted to do more of this work, to spend my time making a difference in the lives of others. I was, however, very time limited as I still had a full-time job. Because my job paid for the mortgage for the property and the upkeep of the horses at this initial stage of the business, I felt it was impossible to reduce my hours at work.

I started to look for ways to create a second income stream. Something that would make me enough money to reduce my hours at my full-time job. This led me to commence an online business in 2018. While the business did not make me enough money to reduce my work hours, it changed my life. It was the first step on my journey of more deeply understanding myself. Personal development training in the business is as important as business training. I was introduced to Rhonda Byrne's book "The Magic," where I learned that gratitude was the key to happiness and manifestation. I began to understand the true meaning of loving myself and loving others. My life became filled with excitement. I also realized that I have an insatiable desire for knowledge and growth.

COVID-19 hit immediately after the pressure of severe drought and the great fires in eastern Australia. I think everyone was exhausted by the ongoing crises, but we continued to do all we could to help make a difference. The best thing that I ever did was give up watching television. Everything on the television was depressing, and I could not put time into my learning if I wasted time watching TV. Once I gave it up, I had so much more time for myself and my growth, and what started to happen was that I could see and connect more within me and in the nature surrounding me. As a result, my desire for knowledge and understanding grew even deeper.

I realize now that we are here to find out who we are, share love, and positively support each other. Reflecting over my life, I can see how every part has played a role in building me into the person I am today. If I had not experienced the things I have lived through, I would not be able to fulfill my purpose today.

My mother had significant mental health issues growing up, which helped me learn to listen, understand and support others.

My son has ADHD and anxiety, and he taught me different perspectives of thinking, learning, and understanding. I wish I had the knowledge I have now back then, as it would have made both our journeys easier, but I needed to learn it for myself. I am so grateful for him, as now I have a much better understanding of those on the autism spectrum.

I am even grateful that I had the experience of living through cancer. Being in that situation enabled me to understand others on this healing journey. Most of all, it helped me understand myself and discover my purpose.

Over the last nine years, since I discovered my purpose, I have grown to find that our path to our purpose continues to evolve. As we learn more, we align closely with our purpose and refine our work. For example, at the beginning of our business, we provided riding lessons, miniature horse visits, and some equine-assisted learning. These physical services support joy, happiness, and personal growth. However, in early 2021, I undertook training to become a Core Healing Breathwork practitioner. This deepened my spirituality and connection with the horses, and I started supporting others in understanding their energy. I utilised my breath to connect with our horses.

Horses are very sensitive to the slightest change in energy, and we can gently direct a horse solely through our breath and body language. This practise enables our clients to understand the power of their energy and ways to manage it effectively. This connected me in 2022 to energy healing through the horses and helped me to understand the horses more deeply. After more than 45 years of horses, it gave me a whole new insight into who horses are. They are not just beasts of burden; they are living sentient beings that can feel our heartbeat at over two meters and our energy to around 16 meters. Horses balance the energy fields in each other's bodies by clearing chakras and energy meridians. This supports the physical and mental health of the horses in the herd. We humans don't realise that our companion horses work to clear our energy blockages by balancing our chakras, helping to support our physical and mental health. I find this truly incredible. No wonder we feel so good after being in a horse's energy.

Our business has grown to incorporate further development in life skills, energy healing through the horses, and personal development through our women's circles. My daughter's focus, in particular, is supporting the owners to understand their horse's communication and enhance the relationship between horse and owner. Our intention for 2023 is to hold more workshops and begin offering retreats.

"Pay attention to the things you are naturally drawn to. They are often connected to your path, passion and purpose in life. Have the courage to follow them."
- Ruben Chavez

The thing about discovering your purpose that I love so much is that as you grow personally and spiritually, your path to your purpose becomes ever more apparent. The universe itself guides us on this journey of discovery.

Our life experiences prepare us for stepping onto our path. As we awaken within ourselves, our way starts to become clearer. The more deeply we connect with who we are, the more deeply we connect with our purpose.

I believe that my purpose in life is to learn what the true meaning of love is and to embody that meaning. This can be done in many ways. The best way to accomplish this is with and through the animals. We then share our purpose with others and support them on their journey of discovery.

There is no one more kind, loving, and wise than the horse to guide us on this journey of discovery. Horses are very patient and know how to bring intuitively to our attention what we need to work on. They help us find the courage and connect deeply to our hearts and soul.

"There is something about the outside of a horse that is good for the inside of a man."
- Winston S. Churchill

Probably the greatest lesson I have learned is that you have your greatest success through the most significant challenges. Those challenges push you to grow, step out of your comfort zone, learn, and become more than you were. While it may be hard while you are in the thick of the experience, keep stepping forward. Just keep taking one step at a time; soon enough, you will be running. Never give up; you never know how close you are to the finish line. There must be a breakdown for you to break through. Reflect with gratitude and see the opportunities that have come to you through those challenges.

Ralph Waldo Emerson was a very wise man. So, I will leave you with this final quote about what success in life is. It is not about just living a life. It is about leaving this earth a better place for having had you in it. This can be in a small way, a very big way, or somewhere in between, and it doesn't matter. It's your life, and here's to your success in seeking and finding your purpose.

"What is success? To laugh often and much; to win the respect of intelligent people and the affection of children; to earn the appreciation of honest critics and endure the betrayal of false friends; to appreciate the beauty; to find the best in others; to leave the world a bit better, whether by a healthy child, a garden patch or a redeemed social condition; to know even one life has breathed easier because you have lived. This is to have succeeded!"

– Ralph Waldo Emerson

"Don't be enticed by success or scared by failure, be captivated by purpose."

~ Bob Goff

CHAPTER TEN

My Story, My Journey Through My Eyes

By Amanda Ray

Discovering your life purpose can be challenging, but it doesn't have to be. Some people wake up daily and repeat the same routine of going to work, coming home, and doing the same thing the next day. Today, more than ever, people feel disconnected and lost, wondering what life's meaning is. They may be questioning, "What's the point?"

Good news: you aren't alone if this is you.

What you believe, whether Western or Eastern philosophy or religion, will influence how you discover your life purpose.

Why is it important to discover your life purpose?

I put this question to my Twitter followers, and I like this description that was shared in response:

> "Our purpose can guide life's emotions; influence behavior, decisions, and goals; offer a sense of direction; and create meaning and a feeling of responsibility for our own choices."

Having a life purpose can help you feel more alive, connected, and less stressed because your life now has meaning. In addition, a clear sense of purpose gives you the motivation and energy to keep moving forward and striving for a better, more fulfilling life.

Note that it's essential to understand what "life purpose" means to you, as it does mean different things to people based on their own experiences, religious beliefs, or cultural upbringing.

Whatever life purpose means to you is the right answer for you; there are no right or wrong answers to your growth journey. So, be guided by your feelings about what suits you.

This is my journey

When I close my eyes, I see myself as a little girl walking along the edge of a rock pool, daydreaming about what she wanted to be when she grew up. But, along the path toward adulthood, these dreams became a distant memory as life would test and challenge me.

For as long as I can remember, my idols were Martin Luther King Jr. and Carl Jung. Martin Luther King Jr. inspired me with his convictions and use of nonviolent actions to achieve equal rights, and his famous "I Have a Dream" speech still moves me today.

He stood for everything good and yet died a violent death.

Carl Jung was the first to develop the theory of the collective unconscious, the belief that all humans are connected to their ancestors through a shared set of experiences. Interestingly, later in life, I would learn that Indigenous Spirituality shares a similar belief.

These two great men changed how people saw the world, and even today, their words still echo throughout humanity as their teachings are still relevant.

Growing up, I learned and researched everything I could about these two great men. The more I learned, the more I kept reinventing myself like a butterfly after each challenge I overcame. But there was always something missing, a piece of the puzzle I couldn't identify that would give my life more meaning—the meaning the little girl dreamed about as she grew up.

Years would pass, and it would be a terrible time when my beautiful dear brother, my living Martin Luther King Jr., died. He promised, "Whenever you see a butterfly, which will be me, looking down and protecting you." My brother's passing made me question our family's history. I wanted to learn more about our grandpa's heritage as he was orphaned after being left on the doorstep of a Salvation Army family's front porch as a baby. There were whispers within the family that his mother was Aboriginal, so I decided to have a DNA test done to confirm once and for all if the whispers were true. The results proved that I did have Indigenous ancestry that was pinpointed to the Cape York region in Far North Queensland.

So began my quest to know more about my ancestry. I wanted to find my great-grandmother, but the question was how? At the time, I was living in Brisbane, Queensland, and my job had just become redundant. This became my how, so, using the opportunity, I started to apply for jobs in Far North Queensland, hoping to end up in the Cape York region eventually.

After several years of living and working in areas up the coast of Queensland, which had me slowly moving further up Queensland towards the Cape York region, I eventually got a job working in an Aboriginal community on Indigenous land.

Although this community is known as Australia's most remote, poor, and violent community, I felt a sense of belonging. It became one of the most significant, life-changing experiences of my life.

Despite the harsh conditions and missing modern conveniences of city life, it was a wonderful way to live. The Aboriginal people don't judge you on how you look or dress; what's inside you is what counts. If you treat them with respect, they will, in turn, treat you with the same respect. They are only too eager to answer if you ask questions about Aboriginal culture and Dreamtime. It's a form of respect if you do ask questions.

I confided in several Aboriginal Elders about my great-grandma and sought their advice. One said, "To understand and know yourself, you must connect with your roots."

The other told me to look at the night sky for guidance, as the night sky keeps a record of my path and life map. It reflects your journey in this life. So, after work, I would sit on my front porch and look towards the sky, amazed at the absolute blackness that engulfed the earth with the sparkle of stars shining down on me. It was while looking into the abyss that everything seemed possible.

Unfortunately, the world was hit with Covid-19 and global lockdown, and the Cape York region became effectively cut off from the rest of Queensland and Australia. Being isolated from the rest of Australia and loved ones was difficult. The community had just gone through riots and a murder that left the town feeling like a pressure cooker about to explode. I also had a broken ankle, and few medical staff were left because of the lockdown, so I couldn't get treatment or even pain relief. But my work colleagues and I had to keep going, working seven days a week to keep the Indigenous safe from Covid-19.

After two years and six months, I left the community. The lockdown and the tragic early death of my nephew made me realize how far away I was from my family. I was emotionally exhausted and wanted to be closer to my daughter. The search for my great-grandmother would have to resume later.

Before I left, I promised my new friends that I would do everything I could to enlighten white Australians on the community's truth—not the truth reported by media, advocates, or city Aboriginals but the truth of Aboriginals living in the country. There is a difference between city Aboriginals and land Aboriginals, just like there is between city people and people who live in the country. Unbeknownst to me, my promise to my friends would lead me to my life purpose.

Driving halfway across Australia

When I left the Aboriginal community, Australia was in the middle of its second Covid-19 lockdown, which made flying difficult. So, I decided to drive. Since every state was in lockdown, the best route was to drive across the top of Queensland, leaving from Cairns into Northern Territory and then down the center of Australia into South Australia.

This meant I would drive in some of the most isolated areas in the Northern Territory, with petrol stations being far and few between towns, in the middle of Australian summer where temperatures could reach 50 degrees Celsius.

My family and friends wanted daily updates via Facebook to track my travels if anything happened.

I took photos as my daily updates, always trying to find angles to show different perspectives. I enjoyed the process and was seeking out great photo opportunities, even going off track to find them. As a result, a passion and natural talent were born that would eventually become part of my life purpose.

Sometimes we can try too hard to discover our life purpose or what we are passionate about.

Trust the journey and let your passion find you.

Returning home to Adelaide

Returning to civilization with modern conveniences was difficult. I found myself looking at everything with new eyes, a new sense of knowing. I also realized that everything I thought I knew, I didn't. I had zero tolerance for modern society. I judged people and thought, "Why are so many people superficial?" or "People seem so rude." I didn't like whom I had become and wanted to return to Far North Queensland. I felt lost again, not knowing what to do and what path to take.

While in Alice Springs on my road trip, I found Dreamtime Reading Cards and the *Aboriginal Dreamtime Journal* by Mel Brown, Ngunnawal Woman, which helped me adjust to civilization and solidify my new insights.

"In search for honesty, first look within."
—Mel Brown, Ngunnawal Woman

The answer was clear: I needed to go deeper to understand myself to truly clear the clutter in my head. But how could I learn to stop judging people? That wasn't me, or so I thought.

"The meeting with oneself is, at first, the meeting with one's own shadow. The shadow is a tight passage, a narrow door, whose painful constriction no one is spared who goes down to the deep well. But one must learn to know oneself to know who one is."
—Carl Jung

Embracing my shadow self and understanding whom I am allowed me to self-reflect and take steps to complete my journey.

My steps

1. Examined my feelings—I started by writing in a journal and drilling down on my feelings by asking myself, "Why do I feel this way?" Then, using the freewriting technique, I kept writing everything that came to me until it became clear.

   The drilling down technique can be useful in negating any negative thoughts and feelings by putting them into perspective.

   For example:

Why do I feel annoyed by people? —Because I used to be like that.

What changed my thinking? —Living in an Aboriginal community and seeing how happy people were because they didn't judge based on outside appearance.

What can I do to live my life that way in the city? —Become self-aware and fully embrace every aspect of my good and ugly personality.

"What we despise in ourselves we project onto others."
—Carl Jung

Our shadow selves are the unwanted parts of our personality that we don't like and hide from ourselves and the world.

Simply put, our words and actions are not congruent, which can cause disharmony with ourselves and our lives, moving us further from our purpose. This experience is expressed in stories like *The Strange Case of Dr. Jekyll and Mr. Hyde*; humans are not one person but two—our conscious personality and shadow self, often battling for control over our minds.

Denying these two selves won't make them disappear, for they remain in our unconscious mind and continue to influence our thoughts, feelings, and beliefs.

I know for me personally, understanding and embracing my shadow self has been beneficial to uncovering my true self and aligning fully with my purpose. Here are some ways to understand and embrace your shadow self:

- Step back and look at your life objectively by pretending you are looking at your life through the eyes of a third person. Notice how you feel about your behaviors and use the drilling down techniques to examine where the feelings came from. For example, are they suppressed feelings from childhood?

Taking notice and observing your actions and behaviors objectively will give you great insight into yourself.

- Be honest with yourself. Uncovering the truth about yourself is hard, but doing so will lead you to become the best version of yourself and guide you toward your life purpose.
- Acknowledge, accept, and forgive yourself. There is no shame, so forgive yourself, for you didn't know better. Now you do, so learn and move forward with your life.

"Our past is for learning;

Our present is for enjoying;

Our future is a combination of our past and present."
—Amanda Ray

2. Examined my dreams—Mel Brown, Ngunnawal Woman, stresses the importance of taking note of our dreams: "… your dreams are providing you with the answers to the issue at hand. Begin to take notice of your dreams, as they are often prophetic. Your dreams give you clear messages, but you still resist because you have trouble trusting yourself and your decisions. Trusting in this decision will turn the tides for you."

   Carl Jung also believed that our dreams were our psyche's attempt to communicate important things. He stated that dreams were an important part of the development of our personality—a process called individuation. Here are a few steps to capture and analyze your dreams:

- Write down the dream using as many details as you can recall, even if they appear unimportant. Details could include the people, location, how old you were in the dream, and the feeling the dream left you with upon waking.
- Make associations or connections with your dream. For example, are your dreams always in a certain location?

Are you always younger or present? Are the same people showing up in your dreams?

- Reflecting on your dream, what's the first thing that comes to mind? Was there a particular symbol or object in your dream?

  I remember one dream in which I was running late for work. Of course, I wasn't in real life, but I couldn't shake the feeling all morning. Finally, after doing the above steps and examining what was happening in my life, the answer was clear: I felt like I was missing out on an opportunity that could help me towards the career I wanted.

  A couple of days before having this dream, I was approached to write a chapter for *Journey of Richness*, but I declined. Fortunately, John contacted me again, and this time, I said yes.

3. Embraced mindfulness—I use photography to quiet my mind. NOTHING ELSE MATTERS when I am off exploring and taking photos; my focus and attention are on what I see. As a result, I feel at total peace and am content with my life in those moments.

Putting it together

After many months of practicing all the above steps and reading more about Dreamtime, my purpose slowly unfolded. I learned many things about myself along the way and believed that the process was also part of my life purpose: to grow into a better version of myself.

However, there was one more step I needed to take.

When I submitted my first draft of this chapter, John rang me and said, "It's good, with some good tips, but it's not personal." As someone used to write corporate reports or meeting minutes, I am a bullet point type. I state the facts and keep emotions out of the picture. So now I had to learn how to write from my experiences—"My Story, My Journey Through My Eyes."

At first, this terrified me, so I did the drill-down technique…

Why am I afraid? —What if people don't like my story?

What's the worst that can happen if they don't? —Nothing, except my ego, would be crushed.

What if people like my story? —That scares me more.

Why? —Because they might want to hear more about my story.

What's bad about people wanting to know more? —Nothing.

What I realized was that it didn't matter if people didn't like my story. If I come from my truth, then that's all that matters. And maybe, there is someone out there who needs to hear the message in this story.

Since returning to Adelaide, many people have asked me to tell my story; they find it inspirational and uplifting. I have also been asked to put together a coffee table book of my photos—my life captured through pictures—and a book of my quotes that I post on Twitter.

The light bulb moment was when I understood that my life purpose is to explore "My Story, My Journey Through My Eyes" through writing, photos, and quotes.

My life has come full circle. That little girl daydreaming on the edge of the rock pool wanted to inspire people, just like her idol Martin Luther King Jr. That little girl had an unshakeable belief in herself that never left her through all the challenges and struggles. She still has that belief today.

I never wanted to conform and be a follower. Instead, like a butterfly, I wanted to flutter my wings and have them felt by as many people as possible.

I want to leave you with two Dreamtime stories that impacted my life and gave me the courage to write my story.

Campfire (extract)

The campfire plays a large part in the lives of traditional Aboriginal Australians. It is also a place where knowledge was shared, and stories told – not only the Dreamtime stories we may be familiar with, but stories of everyday happenings were also retold and enjoyed. There was also an intergenerational transfer of knowledge, as Elders shared their stories with the younger generations and enjoyed watching them grow, learn and try new things.
—Mel Brown, Ngunnawal Woman

"Sharing our stories will allow others to learn from our experiences and to part with our knowledge and wisdom."—Amanda Ray

River (extract)

The river is associated with emotions, which often flow and change direction depending on the obstacles encountered along the way. Sometimes your emotions almost dry up and you find yourself stagnant and stuck. Usually, it will take an outpouring of emotions to fix this – like floods that clean out the debris and your tears and help you let go of emotions and toxins. —Mel Brown, Ngunnawal Woman

"As you progress in your journey, embrace your emotions and feelings. Just like the river, we sometimes have to change direction or stay still to learn the lessons to help us move forward."—Amanda Ray

Acknowledgement of Country

Reconciliation Australia acknowledges Traditional Owners of the Country throughout Australia and recognises the continuing connection to lands, waters, and communities. We pay our respect to Aboriginal and Torres Strait Islander cultures; and to Elders past and present.

Aboriginal and Torres Strait Islander peoples should be aware that this chapter may contain names of people who have passed away.

"The purpose of life is a life of purpose."

~ Robert Byrne

CHAPTER ELEVEN

Living with Purpose

By Yiuvany Aguilar

After the death of my twin daughter Isabella in 2016, my divorce in 2017, and my other twin daughter Camila in 2021, I thought I wouldn't be able to live my life with a purpose anymore. The pain in my heart was so unbearable. My life suddenly had no direction or meaning; it was like a tornado leading to craziness, and sometimes, I did not want to live anymore. Suddenly, my only goal was to survive the day, which seemed difficult and impossible.

Amid the uncertainty, despair, pain, loneliness, and anger, the negative voices in my mind were so strong that I could not escape them; my mind became my jail. But, on the other hand, it was an agonizing voice inside my heart that, from time to time, raised its tone to remind me that I was alive and that my soul still had the opportunity to shine again. Those were moments of insight and reconnection with myself. Through them, I slowly realized I could find my purpose again.

In this chapter, I will share with you how the challenges I experienced led me to explore my purpose and how my life continued to move forward after what I considered my losses.

I invite you to join me in this journey of pain, grief, self-discovery, healing, exploration, and love, and how I slowly found new ways of recovering myself and living life to the fullest again with the angels in my heart and my ex-husband as my best friend.

Facing the Unbearable Reality

Losing a child is the most tragic event someone can experience. After my two-year-old twin daughter Isabella passed away, I felt devastated. I was confused and scared about my future; my sunny days turned dark, and my life changed drastically. As a loving mom, I aimed to care for my daughters best. They were my life, and when I lost Isabella, I felt like I had failed her. I was not ready to start a new life without her; however, life pushed me to be strong and handle my grief better each day.

As the days passed, I felt I did not have enough space or time to grieve. I was confused about how to handle my family's harrowing event. I knew Isabella had her own identity, but at some point, I created the illusion that I could reconnect with Isa through Camila since she was her identical twin sister. Every day, when I missed Isa, I found peace by hugging and kissing Camila. Somehow, this worked perfectly, and my soul found peace.

But life had more surprises for me. A year after Isabella passed away, I got a request from my husband to get divorced. This added more pain to my journey. I started experiencing negative feelings about myself that I hadn't felt before. Suddenly, I felt guilty, blaming myself for everything that went wrong in my relationship. I felt ugly, not sexy, and my confidence faded quickly after he moved out. This new challenge added more disturbance to my life. My emotions were scrambled and distorted; my grief seemed even more impossible to handle. I felt like my purpose had been ripped away from me.

Somehow, I managed my life by trying to survive just one day at a time, going to retreats to explore my inner self. Some days were better than others. Still, my drive was Camila since my oldest daughter Valeria, now in her early twenties, was independent. So slowly, I got used to my new life, sharing fifty percent of Camila's custody with my ex-husband and dealing with separation every time she had to go with her dad.

My stress level was so high during the COVID pandemic that I started panicking because Camila was part of a high-risk population. I did not want her to get the COVID virus; the problem was that my ex-husband and I worked in the healthcare industry. We decided Camila would stay at my house and remain isolated from her dad and me. At that time, Valeria and my niece Andrea were caring for Camila. So, while working on the front line as healthcare workers, my ex-husband and I only interacted with Camilla through video calls. Although serving on the frontline gave me a sense of purpose, those video calls with Camila were heart-wrenching.

Those days were so painful for everyone, but we successfully overcame them. Then, in the middle of the pandemic, Camila started feeling sick. She had no appetite or desire to play as she used to. After several telehealth video calls, the Stanford doctors requested that we take her to the ER. After many labs and tests in the ER, the doctors discovered that Camila's heart function was diminished, and she had to be hospitalized.

After two consecutive, month-long hospitalizations, Camila was discharged with palliative care to be monitored at home. All that time, my ex-husband and I supported each other and cared for Camila, and we cultivated a good relationship. Although Camila needed medical attention, I initially felt that we would get through this together, and gradually, my sense of purpose returned.

But things suddenly became worse. Back in Peru, my family was devastated knowing what was coming. My sisters Lili and Elena visited us; they spent some time providing Camila with the best care possible and cultivated great memories. Unfortunately, after five months of being at home, Camila passed away on May 17, 2021, softly saying her last word: "Bye."

I thought the following days would be the last days of my life. I have never been suicidal; however, I sometimes just wanted to die during that period. I hosted this feeling of heavy emptiness in my chest, a lack of energy that made even breathing hard, and a pain that was killing me silently. Sometimes, waking up was arduous, and I was devastated. My reason for living had been cruelly ripped away from me.

It wasn't until this time that I realized I hadn't grieved Isabella enough or in a healthy way. Suddenly, I felt like I had lost both kids for the first time. I felt guilty that I was unaware that my illusion had covered my grief for Isabella and that I could connect with her through her twin sister. And now my Camila, the source of my connection with Isa, was gone. This caused me so much desperation, guilt, and sadness that I wanted to die, and I didn't want anyone around me because I was broken with no hope for my future.

After Camila's funeral, I had no direction to follow and felt lost in time and space. I was unsure what the plan was for the rest of my life. I never thought I could handle this much pain in one lifetime. The days passed, and my messy life slowly adjusted to a new normal. I managed my pain using all available resources such as therapy sessions, journaling, crying, breathing exercises, joining grieving support groups, contemplating nature, hiking, and spending time with my oldest daughter, family, and friends. Yet, I sometimes felt overwhelmed and just wanted to be alone.

Creating a New Identity

I needed to create a new identity and live purposefully to continue my life. I was made aware of this long before Camila passed away. When she was initially in palliative care, I spent most of my days crying and holding her hands. Sometimes I would cry even while watching her smile and be happy because I knew that soon those smiles wouldn't happen anymore. I was hopeless.

One day, a friend reached out to me over the phone. As soon as I started talking to him, I presented myself as a victim of the circumstances, telling him millions of reasons why I felt devastated and miserable. After acknowledging my feelings, he gave me many valid reasons to change my mental state. He explained that Camila was in a crucial time of her life and that I had choices. I could decide just to keep crying, spending my time in a victim state, or change to a victorious state where I could operate from a place of love and joy, celebrating every day and doing my best to keep cultivating good memories while she was still alive.

He emphasized that this was the perfect time for me to put into practice all the resources I had acquired from my previous training about spirituality. His voice sounded kind but firm at the same time. I was speechless; his advice was not as comforting as other people's, but it was exactly what I needed to hear. He hurt my feelings, which helped me reflect on every word he mentioned. For the first time, I saw clearly that I was creating my memories from a place of resentment and desperation. This shift in perspective empowered me to explore my true purpose in life.

That experience was like an electrical shock to me. My friend was right: I wasted time cultivating more negative emotions and feeding them daily. So, I decided to make some changes to develop a better relationship with my daughter at that stage of her life. I started approaching life differently. I joined a challenge with Tony Robbins called UPW; reviewed my past training with Enrique Delgadillo at "Circulo X"; scheduled an appointment with my therapist; and started eating better, taking showers, exercising, and dancing and singing with my daughter. We took so many pictures and recorded videos, and my energy was so good that it changed not only Camila's energy but also my family's. One day, Camila started walking again and enjoyed spending time in the backyard after being unable to go outside. My heart was filling up with good memories, love, and gratitude. My prayers were to have one more day with my lovely daughter.

After Camila died, all the memories we'd built together fueled my soul and motivated me to keep practicing the routines I had in place. Despite the pain, I slowly started creating a new identity that allowed me to have faith that I could still live my life and rediscover my purpose with my angels in heaven and my heart.

I Had to Win My Mindset First (It's a Mental Game)

While grieving is a process and requires time and space for the emotional wounds to be healed, recovery from grief doesn't automatically happen. This mental aspect was a huge component for me to move forward without feeling miserable all the time. This was the time to renew myself.

There were days when my emotions were up and down, and I felt empty inside, crying for days and feeling the pain so deeply that it paralyzed me. I felt that my life would end at any time, that inner voice in my mind repeatedly asking why this tragedy had happened to me and why I felt so guilty. But what could fill my heart with joy? My established routines were not as intense as when Camila was with me. Instead, the pain was again in my heart, and I started feeling lonely, desperate, and sorry for myself.

During my training with Tony Robbins at UPW, one of my main takeaways was that I needed to pay attention to my inner dialogue. He stated that most challenges are only created in our minds and do not happen in reality. Still, they affect us as if they were happening, negatively impacting our bodies. I could feel this happening physically, mentally, and emotionally. All my inner dialogue and focus were on the pain and the negative emotions. I knew there were moments when feeling and embracing the pain was necessary for my healing process, but I was spending too much time suffering and feeling like a victim. It was not healthy.

One of the resources presented during the Tony Robbins training was the Triad, which is a tool that gives us perspective on our mental state in a specific situation; depending on how we use each element, we can create a great or lousy state, and we can change them consciously in a heartbeat. The elements of the Triad are physiology, focus, and language. So, I aimed to regain control of my mental state and remove myself from this negative prison.

To put this into action, I needed first to identify my negative emotions at a specific moment. Then, I needed to customize my Triad with a positive state. First, for "physiology," I decided to create a specific posture accessible to me at any time, reminding me that I was in control of my life. Just having a simple move commanded my brain that I was in charge. Then, for "focus," I decided to be grateful for the good memories with my daughters and ex-husband and everything they brought to my life. Finally, for "language," I decided to eliminate all bad language or anything that expressed negativity.

Of course, this was a practice I performed every day, but there were days when I felt so miserable. Some days were so confusing. Other days brought more clarity; I realized that the more I practiced the Triad, the greater results I would have. I could feel more gratitude over time, and love displayed its magic and slowly transformed my life.

Physical Movement

Despite the confusion and turmoil that happened quite often, I used my mind intentionally as my ally, and my practice seemed to work. I was managing my mental battles, so I decided to explore my physical strength more. As a holistic nurse, I know how the body, mind, and spirit are connected and that physical activity needs to be in place to create balance. So, if I started strengthening the physical part of my being, a deeper feeling of purpose for living again would grow.

After doing an inventory of what I wanted to explore, I decided to join a hiking group. I loved simultaneously moving my body and spending time in nature. When I did my first official hike, I was so exhausted. I was not in good shape, and I did not like feeling weak while others could go miles without complaining. But my desire was so strong that I kept trying and joined every hike scheduled when I was off from nursing.

Gradually, I started feeling like I was retaking control of my life. But the most critical piece was that I engaged with my pain differently. I had so much respect for myself and my wounds that I started talking about my losses on the trails without being sorry for myself anymore, allowing myself to cry, feel my pain, and move out of the state of suffering when it was needed. My purpose was slowly coming back.

I met amazing hiking friends, and they were willing to plan some hikes when I was off work. That allowed me to challenge myself without pressure because they supported me in every step, especially when we had challenging hikes. Progressively, our friendship became a strong foundation for my healing journey.

Slowly, I felt that hiking opened the door to my heart and let some fresh air in. It was an invitation for me to live again. Every hike was special and unique. Hiking gave me challenges, insights, and a sense of gratitude and love, promoting a connection with God, my daughters, and my emotional wounds. My friends brought joy into my life. My goal to live with purpose was back on track.

Training the Muscle of Faith

Since hiking and focusing on gratitude, I gradually started tapping into my divine soul more often. This place was so peaceful that I wanted to spend more time there.

I had seen that my faith was fragile. My relationship with God had a big gap, and I did not know how to close it. Sometimes, I was very angry at him and occasionally grateful. This battle was in my heart, and I wanted to take care of it.

I had insights and breakthroughs that were giving me more clarity little by little. My puzzle was coming together with the right pieces. For example, I know now that nature connects me with God. Just by contemplating it, I see him revealing his love and power. Gradually, my life purpose started shifting, and I could feel the love of God in my heart shining and giving me hope. My faith got stronger, and God became my main life force again. I started feeling better physically, emotionally, and spiritually. The pain that had caused me so much suffering gradually became my main source of self-discovery, self-awareness, and a complete sense of purpose.

Riding the Roller Coaster of Grief

I was confident about managing my new life and building a new identity. I felt that I had a structure in my life again, a purpose to follow, and now I only needed to work on it. However, it was not that easy; the structure was in place, but it required effort and consciousness, and I could not perform at a hundred percent with the emotional turmoil. There were days I felt the darkness so intense that even waking up was challenging. How could I go hiking like that? Sometimes I had zero drive to do anything, and sometimes I felt like I could conquer the world. It was confusing. On my bad days, my sense of purpose felt like it had been ripped away from me again.

Since grief has its pattern, I decided to follow its rhythm. In the beginning, I was following the chaos and deeply experiencing suffering. Still, later, I discovered that I could take control of how I grieved without denying my pain and, simultaneously, without spending too much time in a state of suffering because it paralyzed me from taking action and living purposefully.

For this to happen, I was required to clearly understand why I wanted to get better, why it was so important to me, and why I needed to see the light in my future. And all my answers were that I needed to improve because I wanted to honor my daughters in heaven. I did not want them to feel guilty about my suffering or unhappiness. Instead, I wanted them to be proud of me. I wanted them to know that they were still my purpose in my life. Also, I wanted to cultivate a healthy relationship with Valeria and be more mindful about how I showed up for her daily.

This fueled my soul to take me out of negativity and hopelessness and live my life with more clarity and love. Slowly and over time, things improved, and I became familiar with the ride of grief. I knew that sadness, disappointment, and frustration were part of the ride. I did not want to deny them, but I did not want to spend too long with those emotions. I could have other feelings as an antidote, like gratitude, love, acceptance, and joy.

Every day became a piece of art; sometimes, my emotions were scrambled, but the magic eventually happened from that chaos, surprising me with new insights. After slowly identifying all the triggers, I learned how to navigate them, strengthening my resolve to live purposefully.

Listen to Them; They Are Not Gone

One day, I participated in a gratitude-guided meditation. The main exercise was to take us imaginarily to a special place and stay in a state of deep gratitude. I pictured my twin daughters in my heart, and my mind took me to the moment they were born. I savored that moment as if it was happening. The love filled my heart, and my whole being benefited from the love created. I realized that my perspective of death was wrong. I had created a separation space between my daughters and me because they were not physically present. This was the reason for my pain. However, through meditation, I could bring them into my heart and feel them if I wanted to. It was just a matter of where I focused my attention. I could access them anytime and anywhere. It was about love; it was not about space or time. Having this connection and love in my life took my purpose for living to another level I never thought possible.

I started feeling my daughters in my heart, and the gratitude worked magically for me. Whenever I thought of and felt my daughters in this space, my heart felt a sense of oneness, fulfillment, peace, and calmness.

One night in my dream, I heard Isabella's voice. Smiling and looking at me, she said: "Mom, why do you feel sad for happy people? I am happy, don't worry." These two sentences still resonate in my ears and help me reflect even more on the grieving process. I started paying more attention to the messages my daughters were sending me constantly. I became more mindful of their presence and love.

Loving Ourselves

There are important factors that can help us discover our purpose. I think that loving ourselves is one of the main keys because if we love ourselves, we can love others. We can create a healing energy for those around us, and our actions of love will speak for us so loudly that we won't need to say a word.

Loving ourselves represents the love we cultivate in our inner world, the quality of our relationship, and the kindness tagging each act or word directed at ourselves. It represents the creation of healthy boundaries to stay away from toxic people or toxic habits and the freedom to say "No" without feeling guilty. It represents the certainty of acting from conviction, not based on what others may think about us. Self-love dares us to step up and take responsibility for our mistakes, knowing they do not define us.

The moment I fell in love with myself, I started expressing profound respect for the person I saw daily in the mirror. I was more loving.

Where Will Purpose Take Me?

According to the Cambridge Dictionary, purpose is why you do something or why something exists. Based on this definition, I thought my life's purpose was to exist. To feel miserable for the rest of my life, with no hope for my future. Fortunately, this thought lost power over time. After losing our loved ones, the first thought that comes to our minds is that we will not see them again because they are gone. This creates a big gap between us and them, and this gap is where the pain and suffering happen. If there is a healthy grieving process, this gap will eventually close with love, meaning the pain will still be there but no more suffering. So, I think that depending on the stage of our life that we are at and the circumstances we face, our purpose is constantly evolving. For example, during that stage of life, when I lost my daughters, my purpose was to get better, get rid of the pain, and smile again. This is so simple and so easy. Still, when you are in deep sadness, healing can be very challenging and requires effort.

Before, when someone asked me about my life's purpose, I thought it had to be something big and involve thousands of people. However, I concluded that my purpose in my life had changed along with my level of consciousness. My purpose in life was completely different before my daughters passed away. I was focused more on the outside happiness than the inside fulfillment, and after they passed away, my focus shifted to my inner self.

One night in my dream, I got chills after I had a clear conversation with my daughter Camila. Looking at me while holding her favorite toy, she told me, "Mom, you are here to take care of yourself and love yourself; please do not forget that." After that, she disappeared. I got scared because I could not see her anymore. Still, suddenly again, her sweet voice resonated in my heart, saying: "You know what is next? The suffering will go away, and you will become a voice that some people need to hear, and you will give a voice to the voiceless because pain paralyzes them. Be focused."

After she finished, I woke up, and my whole body experienced a light bath. I could feel white waves going down from my head to my toes. It was a fantastic experience, and at the same time, I was so excited that I could still see my daughter. My heartbeat was fast; I was awake and felt Camila beside me. I could almost feel her breath, and a sense of calmness invaded my heart. I was excited about her message and wrote it down in my little notebook on the nightstand as soon as possible.

I am not the person I was before I had my daughters. I'm living with more purpose. Because of that experience of loss, pain, suffering, self-reflection, love, discipline, and spiritual connection, my level of consciousness has expanded, and my perspective of life has changed drastically. I know that when we act from a place of love, magical things will happen in our lives. Love is a universal healing tool; it connects us with those no longer physically with us, and we can feel their energy stronger than ever.

I know that the more I cultivate love, the more miracles I witness, which is a great way to live and connect with our divine self. I know that I am God's work in progress, and for now, my purpose is to GROW FULLY ALIVE THROUGH THE GIFTS OF LOSS and work daily to keep my mind, body, and spirit in harmony.

In the past, I would consider that I lost my daughters; however, nowadays, I know that I never lost anything. They are still the best—God's gift. They are the stars that guide my new journey every day.

After I let go of all my expectations, my daughters returned to my heart in divine energy and love, and they will rest there forever.

Namaste

"Your purpose in life is to find your purpose and give your whole heart and soul to it."

~ Buddha

CHAPTER TWELVE

Be True to Yourself

By Annette Korolenko

"To thine own self be true."
William Shakespeare

No matter where you are, unexpected adventures help you rediscover your purpose and realign your soul.

How much of our life is determined by circumstances beyond our control, a fate not chosen by us, drifting like a sailboat pulled off course? When our soul's purpose is calling to us, like the gentle wind to our sails, we can choose to reach our destiny by adjusting those sails to the winds of our Spirit, guiding us back to our soul's purpose.

The quest to learn more, research, and find answers is motivated by curiosity and the world's wonder. It's exhilarating to reach our highest possibility with passion and inner drive by overcoming personal limitations and circumstances, to attain what you yearn for.

Remember your childhood to ask yourself, "What made your heart sing?"

Every experience, whether different jobs, travels, or people you meet, could have meaning in your life, leaving clues to remind you of whom you were meant to be.

Do you remember watching a movie and thinking it could have been you?

Do the lyrics of a song echo how you are feeling? Have you read a passage in a book that changed your life? Or has a painting evoked profound emotion within you?

When something beautiful moved me so indescribably, I couldn't find words, whether it was instrumental music, song lyrics, a work of art, or poetry. I would get chills when touched by the depth of what I was feeling and experiencing. Spontaneous, golden threads would connect me to a higher part of myself, later aligning and revealing my purpose.

I remember, as a child, observing the environment around me. I would wonder while watching, listening, and feeling, trying to make sense of the world. I was eager to learn how to read and write, and when I did, I found my favorite place, the library. In the library, I discovered a great passion for finding answers. Reading was my key to the world.

At home, my mother began sharing her stories of healing and transformation. Her story was from the eyes of herself, as a 9-year-old, in Poland when World War II broke out, witnessing the evils of humanity and the good in the human Spirit of man. From her experience of hunger, she enjoyed cooking, feeding the hungry, and offering a place to stay in our home. She had discovered her life purpose and later opened a tiny neighborhood restaurant to feed people. It was a cozy atmosphere for neighbors to gather to enjoy food, music and tell stories of their diverse homelands.

She continued with the story of her two brothers, my uncles, whom I had never met, who were hidden heroes in WWII that risked their lives helping countless strangers, both Poles, and Jews, in concentration camps that were next up for extermination. Upon returning to rescue more, they were caught and shot as political prisoners. All the stories of hidden heroes who risked their lives to save strangers set a high bar as role models for me to look up to when pondering my life's purpose.

My father's story followed. At the age of 12, he attended a music conservatory. After leaving the building five minutes late, he was arrested for breaking curfew, interrogated, then sent to a concentration camp. He found the accordion of a gypsy who had died. When he started playing his heart out, the beautiful music moved the guards to spare his life.

After the war, he continued his passion as a musician. He played in a band and followed his dream to open a music studio to enrich children's lives by teaching them to play various instruments. He had always known that music was his purpose.

Listening to these stories opened my heart with a wave of compassion, inspiring me to help others. Then I became curious to explore other cultures and stories further, igniting the spark to travel abroad.

I started journaling in primary school. Writing was my friend and confidante when working through questions and searching for finding answers. But unfortunately, I didn't always understand the whys of what motivates human behavior. Thus began my self-discovery.

In my journal, I wrote: "What would make me happy and give my life meaning? Then I explored my passions by listing them and why they made me happy.

I soon started recording these family stories to honor the hidden heroes of everyday life; for it was in others' stories that I reflected on myself and my purpose of whom I wanted to become.

In these moments of reflection, I had an epiphany; I knew that I wanted to be a writer and to be of service. I found joy in school by writing essays, stories and writing for the school newspaper.

My parents asked me to accompany their friends and neighbors to translate at doctor visits, court appearances, and the like. My passion for the library helped me to search for the answers in books, so people could understand the facts needed to make important life decisions.

I love helping immigrants aspire for more by reaching out of their comfort zone without being limited by language barriers. I would ask them questions to help them look within and rediscover their purpose. I encouraged them to go to school and change jobs to match their purpose. I offered to help guide them in both for free.

I introduced each person to the free programs at the library, including English lessons. Then I led them to an essential tool to help them discover their purpose within a job. The tool was a volume of books titled "Occupational Employment and Wage Statistics," published annually by the U.S. Bureau of Statistics. In these books were general career fields listed by groups. Within each group were related subfields, education prerequisites, salaries, and the demand in those fields.

It was very fulfilling to watch their futures change before my eyes. In doing so, it inspired me also to become a Life Coach.

My parents had decided I would become a doctor or lawyer because I had been in the position of a translator since first grade, exploring these fields. But my time spent in the library was reading books and following my passion for learning new things, exploring different topics, and reading about other countries.

Coming from the melting pot of Chicago with so many cultural influences, I wanted to explore the world.

I learned there were infinite possibilities in life. There was a guiding force, like the winds of the sea, pushing my sailboat forward. It was up to me to adjust those sails and steer the rudder of the boat to change course to reach my destination and fulfill my life's purpose.

I chose to make decisions, not conforming to the opinions of others and what everyone else expected of me. I had to follow what became my motto:

"To thine own self be true."

The golden thread of my soul's purpose was guiding me from a deep knowing within.

The fulfillment of spiritual needs brings meaning to my life while exploring my many passions. Eventually, that golden thread intertwined with the golden thread of others seeking the same. That synergy between myself and others created magic in living the life of my dreams.

I was ready to embark on a journey of discovery. To give up the familiar to create a vibrant new future. I prepared to give up the past to live in the present moment of each day, starting an adventure while taking only the adaptable skills that helped continue my purpose.

I searched to find my tribe.

Fast forward a few years ahead as an adult at 19, after I had reached my initial epiphanies in my hometown Chicago, I had to readjust the sails of my boat to steer through life's storms toward a different land from where I was born…

I had only a small idea of where my destination would be to stay for several years, and I chose to be open-minded and explore other countries to see if I could serve my purpose there.

I prepared ahead by buying a couple of travel guidebooks. The series was written and researched by Harvard students called *Let's Go Europe*, with all the information you need in each country to get around, including mini maps of major cities.

I traveled across the ocean in a passenger ship to Europe, bringing my car and all the money I had saved from working three jobs. After nine days of travel, I disembarked in Holland to begin my drive to Paris, France, to test the waters to see if I could serve my purpose there. Although Paris was gorgeous, speaking French did not come easily. The city was overcrowded with tourists and locals jamming traffic every day. Room rental prices were high, and the cost of living was much higher than in the U.S. for gas, food, and essentials. I only stayed one week before driving four hours to visit distant relatives who had emigrated to a small town.

I arrived to greet my relatives in a small farm town outside of Metz, Avignon, surrounded by beautiful landscapes of hills, farms, and wheat fields with colorful wildflowers.

They graciously allowed me to stay for two months. During my stay, I worked seasonally in a field of tree orchards picking apples and other fruits to make up for my losses in Paris.

Then I said my goodbyes and left for the port city of Genoa, Italy, a smaller tourist location with the possibility of finding work.

Renting a room was hundreds of dollars cheaper, with a lower cost of living, and the Italians were very warm and friendly. I was happy that there were many meaningful opportunities for teaching conversational English and working freelance with tourists as a guide. I fell in love with Genoa's breathtaking view of the sea. I imagined someday buying a shack closer to the sea to write books in. I even daydreamed of purchasing a real sailboat to rent out to tourists. But that was a far-off dream that would take at least ten years because there wasn't enough work to advance.

Upon leaving Genoa, I realized all the experience and daydreaming weren't for naught. I knew I would someday write a story about that time that was etched in my memory.

I decided to drive to my final destination on the list, Poland. Little did I know that this place would strengthen the golden thread of my soul's purpose. I was hesitant at first to live in a communist-controlled country. The cost of living on everything was only 10% of the U.S. Earnings were low, only $20 per month. But my saved money was worth more, in the long run, to get settled for a few years.

I knew what my purpose was and why I chose to live there. My dream had always been to study at the 13th-century University in Krakow. I was passionate about teaching English and translating to help people improve their lives. In addition, I wanted to study psychology to inspire and empower others to find their purpose and live the life they were meant to live.

When I found out my application was denied, I was disheartened. Even though I applied for residency, I would have to attend as an American paying tuition in U.S. dollars, which I could not afford.

That night, I gazed up at the midnight sky in deep reflective thought, questioning,

"Why are there obstacles in my path for my dreams to materialize?" I hadn't realized God had a greater plan for me to serve His purpose.

The next morning something nudged me to turn on the radio. There was an ad blaring seeking bi-lingual applicants to study for one year to receive accreditation for working with foreigners as a tour guide. I was excited to start classes.

One year went by quickly. Finally, the day came when I completed school exams and went to pick up my accreditation papers. A visitor came to the school, who was often present listening in on lectures. That day, he tapped me on the shoulder and handed me his business card with the words, INTERPRESS - International Press Agency." He offered me a job working with foreign reporters as an interpreter.

That day was pivotal in my life. A cascade of jobs was offered. The golden thread continued beyond everything I could ever have imagined for myself at God's speed.

And then, just like that! The stars had aligned! My heart, soul, and mind were one. That golden moment of lucidity came over me like a wave revealing the answer to my quest. This is what I was meant to do...

The rediscovery of my purpose at Interpress evolved into personal growth, working with reporters on stories ranging from historical, scientific, and political events to inspiring everyday humanitarian stories.

From this connection also came the opportunity to work on a foreign film as a translator and production assistant on location in the medieval town square of Krakow. Participating in various phases in creating this movie and watching the spiritual premise come to life enhanced my life. It inspired me to consider, in addition to writing books, the medium of screenplays for movies and documentaries to write for and reach a larger audience to do something meaningful. I still wanted to be a Life Coach and help people in all the ways I served up to this point. I also thought about creating online coaching courses as an added purpose.

As I thought about all the different stories with the reporters, I realized that being part of the stories led me to evolve as a writer.

I was saddened when I thought of returning to the U.S. This unforgettable journey of self-discovery in Renaissance Krakow permeated my soul.

I came to understand the Renaissance movement through Krakow. My senses were heightened by experiencing the indescribable beauty of this medieval city through its inspiring Romanesque architecture. The exploration of ideas, creativity, higher thought, and the arts was revealed in the manifested achievements of man inspired by spirit. This is a force we can all connect to at any time.

After ten years of flying back and forth to Chicago, I decided to return to the U.S. to care for my parents, who were elderly.

I continued helping people in Chicago as I had done since childhood. By following my purpose in different ways, I hoped to make a difference in someone's life to pursue their purpose too.

The golden thread that led me to join an online writing group, "Your Book Writing Breakthrough," with John Spender & Guests, was the beginning of learning golden nuggets of wisdom from John Spender's classes.

The writers came from different countries across the ocean, bringing diverse flavors and styles from their homeland, creating magic in their stories. As a result, a special circle formed of friendships while encouraging and supporting one another to freely write from our imaginations.

This experience jumpstarted me on the fast track to writing. I was fortunate to be invited to co-author three International Best Sellers in John Spender's series of *Journey of Riches*, for which I am grateful and ecstatic to be writing.

Within these classes, I could draw from my memory and bring to life my daydreaming in Genoa into a story called "Dreamers" and other stories reminiscing about my love of my mini-Renaissance experience in Krakow.

I didn't believe I could create fiction stories. It's amazing what you can create in the right environment, even stories of fiction, when you follow your purpose…

From the beginning, answers to questions came like a whisper in a gentle breeze, revealing my purpose. And now, they come back like an echo, reminding me of my calling.

In the asking, questioning, and searching that answers are revealed...

I could navigate my life by trusting my intuition by following my North Star.

I made the choice to follow my intuition by taking action. I was always led by a guiding force to unexpected happenings, making desires come true...

At the beginning of your path to purpose, ask questions by journaling and open yourself up to receive answers from your voice within; by listing your passions that give meaning to what you value with the reasons why, you may discover your purpose. Write down what gives you energy and a zest for life. Passion is connected to purpose.

When you sleep, keep paper and pen by your bed to record your dreams first thing in the morning. Then your subconscious may reveal what you truly desire.

Some people find inspiration in nature, others in the library reading the wisdom in books. Both are great places to explore.

Travel to a new place. Go off the beaten path to places undiscovered by tourism that aren't in guidebooks; there are so many hidden gems to explore.

Go out and about in your neighborhood. Instead of turning the corner left, turn right, seeking unexpected happenings. You never know if you will encounter a random stranger who could initiate a conversation that could change your life.

Explore your town for free art festivals, outdoor concerts, and art museum days. Stop to listen to the originality of street music. Immerse yourself in art and different genres of music. Music and art raise vibrational frequencies to connect with your spirit.

Sign up for a class that you would typically not choose. Thumb through college catalogs for random ideas that may ignite a spark leading you to something else. Be open to possibilities in finding your purpose.

Expand your horizons. Be bold and daring to start new adventures.

These activities will stimulate your imagination and raise your frequencies to match what you are drawn to, showing you clues.

Spontaneous golden threads will connect you to a higher part of yourself by raising your vibrations, aligning and revealing your purpose…

We are all part of something much greater than ourselves…

"Two roads diverged in a wood, and
I took the one less traveled by, and
that has made all the difference."
~ Robert Frost

“The purpose of life, after all, is to live it, to taste experience to the utmost, to reach out eagerly and without fear for newer and richer experience.”

~ Eleanor Roosevelt

CHAPTER THIRTEEN

The Maze Of Discovering Your Purpose

By John Spender

Purpose and its Impact on Personal Fulfillment and Motivation

I've worked as a writer and publisher for years, and the evolution of this book series superseded any expectations I may have had when I started. At first, publishing a book was quite daunting, and I certainly didn't think that book publishing or even writing was a part of my purpose. I still remember being a nine-year-old boy, not knowing how to read and write at a basic level. Who knew my purpose would be to help others share their inspiring, uplifting stories?

After launching the first book in the *A Journey of Riches* series, I swore I would never launch another book. I was working as a coach after moving my practice from an office to online through video calls in 2013 in Bali. The mentor supporting my business transition suggested I run a six-month coaching program and include a book bonus. The ten people that came on board would have the opportunity to feature in a multi-author book. I thought of having no publishing experience and figured I'd ask my friends how they published their books when the time was right.

"The meaning of life is to find your gift.
The purpose of life is to give it away."
~ Pablo Picasso

It was a much bigger project than I expected, taking almost two years to publish the first one. If I weren't receiving Facebook messages from friends asking if I would do another one, I would have focused on group coaching instead.

I love the freedom that an online business gives you. Moreover, most people, at their core, want to impact someone else's life positively. Knowing you are making a difference in someone else's life is fulfilling. Initially, I ran coaching programs and released two more books the following year, then four the year after, and doubled each year after. Sure enough, clients, peers, and friends began asking me if I would help them publish their books or, in many cases, book series. Naturally, I phased out of coaching and focused on publishing non-fiction books exclusively. So, what is the purpose of my work? And if I spend most of my day, not to mention my life, managing books, what is my life's purpose?

Allow me to answer that question with a question. Have you heard of the IKEA effect? It turns out that this successful Swedish corporation, present in major metropolitan areas worldwide, demonstrates a phenomenon that many are unaware of. The IKEA effect is that we tend to place a higher value on things when actively involved in manufacturing or assembly. In his book, IKEA Edge, Dahlvig shares the concept of IKEA, not just as another furniture company in the market. He talks about the organizational culture and how the producers work together and are aligned while maintaining their company's style and purpose. The purpose that drives IKEA is personal fulfillment, meaning, and motivation from the beginning of the production chain to the customer. This leads to the following:

Shareholders and the entire human capital of the company are happy.

People enjoy their work.

Customers enjoy shopping in their stores.

Customer and employee retention.

"Should the overriding purpose of the corporate community be to maximize shareholder and managers' wealth, as seems to be the predominant view within the business community? Or should business contribute more substantially to a better world," said Anders Dahlvig in IKEA Edge.

So, how do we define our purpose in life? The simplest way is to follow a four-step process, from the general to the particular.

Step 1: Define your focus. This step is the most important because it requires honesty about who and how you are. It's a behind-the-scenes look where you place all your conscious and unconscious spotlights. For example, where do you spend the most time, energy, and money? These are key indicators of what you value and where you should focus. When we are out of alignment with what lights us up, we can dwell in a negative perspective, often victimizing ourselves, unable to see any light.

Step 2: I invite you to ponder this question, "What resonates with your focus?" This question aims to evaluate your present and project your future. You choose happiness as your focus; define what happiness means to you. Maybe it's in harmony with your family? Living in the mountains? Immersing yourself in nature? Having financial stability? Whatever it is, it serves us best when we define it.

Step 3: What activities align with your focus? Is it dancing? Traveling? Sharing? Writing? Community? Notice that these are verbs because they are actions. Knowing your innate skills and qualities, you can draw your map toward your life's purpose. One that lights a fire under your belly with challenge, fulfillment, and reward. I like to travel while having a sense of purpose. So, one of the questions I asked myself was, "How can I combine travel with my purpose?"

Step 4: Recognition, acceptance, and detailed orientation. This is where you identify your innate skills, qualities, and characteristics and use them to your advantage. You draw your map toward your mission and your life purpose. It's imperative, to be honest with yourself, recognize your lights and shadows, and use them to your advantage.

I invite you to make yourself a cup of your favorite drink and have a deeper conversation with yourself. Wrap a pencil and paper around it and divide the paper into two columns. The first column will be titled "to keep, improve, and keep in mind," and the second will say "to recognize, accept, and improve."

While sipping your drink, look in the mirror and recognize your innate skills, qualities, and characteristics that require little effort to succeed. Write them down in the first column. They are your lights. In the second column, write down those characteristics and skills that are more challenging. These are qualities that you would like to develop.

After completing this simple self-exploration, you'll understand what lights you up, what you value, and what you want to focus on.

"The two most important days in life are the day you are born and the day you discover the reason why."
– Mark Twain

Unconsciously, people are willing to invest their time and effort in the IKEA experience because it's fulfilling, which is the meaning of life. It's like a maze, offering many possibilities in an environment that provides just a few shortcuts by design. It renews itself regularly and enlightens us in every corner if we are interested.

The purpose of life isn't to find a destination or a particular place but to make the most of our experience, the experience of life. Even if you believe in reincarnation, the way life presents itself, the facts, the environment, the friends, the family, the job, the studies, and the current lifestyle are so many factors that the experience is unique and unrepeatable.

Section 2: Signs of a purposeful life

Now that we know that our purpose in life isn't a thing but the experience of achieving it and living it, there are five signs to help us recognize its existence…

1. We have a sharp vision. This doesn't mean that all of our problems and worries disappear, but when we have a clear goal, we can better plan and make the right decisions to achieve what we want because we know what we want to achieve. These signs may include a sense of meaning and fulfillment in one's work, relationships, and other aspects of life. Think Elon Musk and his vision for Tesla. The problems and challenges he overcomes daily lead him to achieve his mission. A big vision drives you to be a better version of yourself to reach your full potential in fulfilling your purpose.

2. We are motivated. Our passion drives our purpose, and this, in turn, leads to action. Once we discover our purpose in life, we are energized. We desire to move forward and rise above because we know everything we do aligns with our goals. This positively impacts our emotional state and even our physical and mental health.

At the Marcus Institute for Aging Research in Boston, researchers Ph.D. Patricia A. Boyle, Ph.D. Aron S. Buchman, Ph.D. Robert S. Wilson, Ph.D. Lei Yu, Ph.D. Julie A. Schneider, Ph.D., and MD David A. Bennett have teamed up to study the "Effect of Purpose in Life on the Relation Between Alzheimer's Disease Pathologic Changes on Cognitive Function in Advanced Age." And that's just one of the benefits of having a sense of life: it also prevents diseases like depression and anxiety. As a result, we are more likely to engage in activities that promote wellness and self-care.

3. It helps us prioritize. Individuals living on their purpose may also feel a sense of inner peace and contentment as they can focus on what truly matters to them. Having found our purpose in life,

we know what is essential and what isn't. Therefore, we can act accordingly and focus on the truly important things.

This doesn't mean our purpose won't change the form or priorities, but the underlying values are usually the same. For example, I had a landscaping company for 11 years and transitioned into speaking, coaching, writing, and the book-publishing business. On the surface, my purpose of creating functional outdoor spaces looks different from publishing books.

However, the underlying values are almost the same. In landscaping, I aimed to give people outdoor spaces to enjoy, feel inspired, and entertain. With book publishing, I help people to express themselves, inspiring others to live with more hope and self-confidence.

The form of our purpose changes but the core drivers that light us up don't. So, when we prioritize our values, we are in harmony with our soul's purpose.

4. Pave our way. When we pursue a goal, our lives take on meaning. This is how we take the reins of our lives and learn to enjoy the experience.

Reflecting on personal satisfaction and joy in life is crucial to living purposefully. When we are living our lives with a sense of purpose, we tend to feel more satisfied and fulfilled. We have a sense of meaning and direction, which allows us to make decisions and actions that align with our purpose. In my experience, the universe offers us answers to help us out when we have clear goals and intentions.

Additionally, individuals living their purpose tend to experience greater well-being and happiness. This is because their purpose gives them a sense of direction and motivation, which can help them overcome challenges and find joy in everyday life.

Emphasizing the importance of self-awareness and introspection is also key. When we can understand our values, passions, and strengths, we can better align our actions and decisions with our purpose. This self-awareness can also help us to overcome challenges. Ultimately, living purposefully requires a deep understanding of oneself and a commitment to personal growth and development.

Section 3: Aligning our purposes

Understanding the connection between values, passions, and purpose is crucial for whoever wants to live a more purposeful life. When we align our values and desires with our purpose, we are more likely to experience a sense of meaning and fulfillment.

Reflecting on personal values and how we relate to one's purpose is a significant step in aligning with one's purpose by understanding what is most important to us. In addition, exploring passions and interests that can be integrated into one's purpose is also important. Three key elements help us align ourselves with our purpose:

1. Balance and autonomy - This is the ability to do things harmoniously with the environment. It is not about running off tomorrow and becoming entrepreneurs or freelancers; it's about finding a balance between the path of the labyrinth we think is laid out in life and our purpose. We are social beings, we're connected to our environment, and although the world doesn't revolve around us, a micro-world cooperates with the outside in each of us. It is pure symbiosis. Remember that your experience is unique. We must be aware that how we live is up to us; we are the primary energy source to move forward.

2. Breakthrough Diagnosis - It refers to noticing changes and progress that help motivate us. Likewise, progress allows us to monitor and recognize when we need to make improvements and when we should continue a specific path. I recommend that occasionally, perhaps once a year, you analyze whether your actions, work, relationships and even the books you read are moving you forward or away from your path. Love yourself. You are valuable, essential, and worth investing in.

3. Clear Vision - This helps us connect with what we want in our lives, values, and missions. If our actions align with our life purpose, we will have more power to achieve them.

Highlighting the importance of aligning actions and decisions with one's purpose for authenticity. Living on purpose requires individuals to be true to themselves and their values. When individuals align their actions with their purpose, they can live authentically and with integrity.

Section 4: Embracing Opportunities

Before I moved to Bali in January 2013, I had a goal of becoming an international trainer in the personal development field. I first set this intention in 2010 at T. Harv Eker's Enlighten Warrior training camp in Malaysia. It was an incredible five days of transformational processes, and with one of them, we set an intention of what we wanted to do next with our lives. Armed with our sense of purpose, we broke into pairs with a thick iron rod. The idea was to stand opposite your partner, placing the steel rod with a rubber tip on the ends between you. We then put the rod in the middle of our throats while repeating our purpose, walking toward each other.

If I hadn't seen the two women trainers demonstrate from the stage that it could be done, I would never have believed it. The steel rod was an inch and a half thick. You couldn't bend it with your hands, and I saw many participants try. The energy in the room of 300 people was one of excitement and nervousness. I stood before my buddy for the process, a fellow named Otto. He is half-Samoan from his mother's side and half-German from his father's side and stands at six feet, six inches, with a heart full of purpose. I felt much smaller even though I'm six-four, standing opposite each other with the steel rod resting in the pit of our throats and staring into each other's eyes with commitment.

Everyone was cheering, and the atmosphere felt very supportive; we were pumped and ready to commit to our dream purpose. When the trainer shouted, "Go!" we focused on our intention in our minds, eyes staring at each other as we walked forward until there was nothing between us except a bent rod. What a mind-blowing experience that left me feeling full of belief in my goal and purpose of becoming an international trainer. Otto, who ran a martial arts school, wanted to create women's self-defense online programs and retreats, which he achieved three after the training camp. Through many peaks and valleys, I moved to Bali, teaming up with a US NLP training company running their training in Southeast Asia, mainly in Singapore.

After renewing my second three-month contract, I decided that working for someone else and running training sessions wasn't for me. I enjoyed helping people but not the long hours indoors. I liked the location independence that coaching gives you; the reward of helping someone else achieve their dream was liberating. I had no real plan after I left, I just knew it was time, and that's when I met my mentor, and she helped me to launch my new coaching program, which set me on the path of becoming a writer and publisher.

Rarely is discovering our purpose a straight line or an easy endeavor to achieve, but this is how we become better versions of ourselves. It's like going into an IKEA store for a new entertainment unit. It is like a maze where our steps are delineated. There can be many distractions as we pass the home decoration department or the office furnishings. You must go through all these departments. Our eyes can easily get lost among the different items while the mind forgets the entertainment furniture. Instead, it shouts things like "I can do that," "That's the perfect shelf for the bathroom," "Those are the perfect utensils for the grill," and "I can assemble this room set myself"... And so, the mind flies away.

The same goes for opportunities: they are there, aligned with our purpose, but it is a miracle that anyone points them out. We need to recognize them, even if it means taking a detour or not knowing which is the best path. Embracing opportunities is a crucial part of living on purpose. However, fear and self-doubt often discourage people from taking risks and stepping out of their comfort zones.

Pursuing new experiences that align with one's purpose can be intimidating, but the rewards are well worth it.

One way to overcome fear and self-doubt is to focus on the potential for growth and learning. Every opportunity, whether it leads to success or failure, provides a chance to expand one's purposeful journey. Individuals can discover new strengths, interests, and passions that fuel their purpose by taking calculated risks.

It's also important to recognize that opportunities come in different forms. Sometimes, they may not be obvious or require hard work and dedication. However, you can find opportunities that align with your purpose by staying open-minded and persistent. Living on purpose requires a willingness to embrace uncertainty and take risks. It can be scary, but the journey toward purposeful living is often filled with unexpected opportunities and moments of growth. By stepping out of one's comfort zone and being open to new experiences, you can create a fulfilling and meaningful life that aligns with your purpose and values.

Section 5: Embodying Commitment

Living on purpose requires a high level of commitment and dedication. It is a lifelong journey that requires perseverance, resilience, and overcoming challenges and obstacles. However, when we align our actions and decisions with our purpose, the good news is that we experience a genuine commitment and intrinsic motivation that fuels our journey.

Commitment to living on purpose is about changing your identity by achieving personal goals and making a meaningful difference in the lives of others. When a sense of purpose drives individuals, they are more likely to be initiative-taking and move towards creating positive change in the world around them. They surround themselves with supportive people with similar values, and they never quit on themselves.

People who are committed to their purpose are better equipped to navigate challenges with resilience and determination. They understand that setbacks and failures are opportunities for growth and learning and use these experiences to fuel their purposeful journey.

Living on purpose requires a purpose-driven commitment that fuels perseverance. Even though it cannot be achieved overnight, it is worth the effort.

Section 6: Awaken an Inner Drive That's Motivating and Inspiring

This is about how to awaken an inner motivating and inspiring drive. It entails exploring the internal drive and motivation of living on purpose. It involves tapping into the passion and inspiration that propel us toward our purpose. It also consists in harnessing the purpose to ignite inner fire and energy.

Living on purpose means understanding one's values, strengths, and goals. It involves knowing what brings joy and fulfillment and pursuing activities that align with those things.

One must connect with our passion and inspiration to tap into this internal drive and motivation. This involves identifying the things that bring us joy, excitement, and a sense of purpose and the things that magnetize us. It could be a hobby, a cause we care deeply about, or a profession that aligns with our values and strengths. Once people identify their passion and inspiration, they can harness purpose to ignite their inner fire and energy.

Section 7: Fulfillment of Self and Others

The pursuit of a purposeful life can have a profound impact on both our well-being and others' lives. Living purposefully and passionately makes us more likely to experience meaning and fulfillment. This can lead to improved mental and emotional well-being and enhanced life satisfaction. In addition, by understanding the impact living on purpose can have on our well-being, we can make more intentional choices about how we spend our time and energy.

Living with passion and purpose can also positively impact others' lives. We inspire and motivate others to discover and pursue their purpose when we are passionate about something. This is their passion and goal. It is paramount to remember that we are all connected, and we, as independent individuals, are just a grain of sand in the sea. Still, we build the universe together, so pursuing our life experiences in peace and harmony with our environment is imperative. By making a meaningful difference in others' lives through purpose-driven living, we can create a ripple effect that spreads positivity and joy throughout our communities.

Section 8: Gaps and Values

Along our life's journey, we encounter a variety of situations that have the potential to affect our perspectives and beliefs, from moments of triumph to setbacks and loss.

These experiences can leave us feeling incomplete or disconnected from our true selves, but they also provide opportunities for growth and self-discovery. By confronting our gaps, we can better understand our passions. Through our struggles, we gain valuable insight into our strengths and weaknesses, and this self-knowledge helps us identify our values and purpose.

Therefore, we must take the time to reflect on our gaps and values to navigate the journey of discovering our purpose. As a result, we gain clarity and focus on what matters most to us. We can purposefully identify and pursue our passions, leading to a more fulfilling life. Remember, discovering our purpose can be more like a maze than a straight line, but we will find our way with patience and perseverance.

References; Anders Dahlvig Date uploaded (2020) "The IKEA Edge: Building Global Growth and Social Good at the World's Most Iconic Home Store." McGraw-Hill.

Dr. Patricia A. Boyle, Ph.D., Dr. Aron S. Buchman, MD, Dr. Robert S. Wilson, Ph.D., Dr. Lei Yu, Ph.D., Dr. Julie A. Schneider, MD, and Dr. David A. Bennett (2012); "Effect of Purpose in Life on the Relation Between Alzheimer Disease Pathologic Changes on Cognitive Function in Advanced Age"; Published in final edited form as Arch Gen Psychiatry. (Link https://www.ncbi.nlm.nih.gov/pmc/articles/PMC3389510/)

“If you can’t figure out your purpose, figure out your passion. For your passion will lead you right into your purpose.”

~ Bishop T.D. Jakes

AUTHOR BIOGRAPHIES

Jane Forkert

CHAPTER ONE

Jane's life purpose is writing especially scriptwriting. She graduated in 2015 with a BA in Writing Studies, and although it took a few years to succumb to her heart, she now has numerous projects on the go.

Jane was born in Waikato Hospital, New Zealand, unable to breathe; she was given a tracheostomy, and in 1987, major surgery scarred her vocal cords. No amount of laser surgery helped. A horse called Johnny did, and he tells his story in her upcoming book *My Animals Speak* – an autobiographical account through the voice of her animals.

The mother of three sons, she raised the boys on her own. The middle one provides her latest scriptwriting project:

Autumn Falls – a screenplay from the perspective of an inmate's mother.

Jane is an animal communicator and loves working with horses. Her soon-to-be-released book, *Listen. Just Draw a Circle* shares the process of hearing your animal.

Jane also coaches, serving her clients in powerful one-to-one sessions that provide the structure for living successful heart-led experiences in business, relationships, and life. She is currently writing a book to support her coaching; *Short-circuit Your Bullshit* – a self-help guide to the most efficient way of dealing with the egoic structure and landing you smack bang in your heart (life purpose).

Website: www.happilyheart.com

Email: happilyeq@gmail.com

Emma Flowers

CHAPTER TWO

Emma Flowers was born and raised in England and has had a passion for writing since childhood. In the early days as a young adult, while trying to figure out who she was and what she wanted to be, Emma worked in various jobs, like hospitality, sales and marketing, and other corporate duties. She also speaks two languages, English and Italian, which came in very handy in her last job.

It wasn't until Emma started a family that she realised her true purpose was to write. The turning point was when she immigrated to Australia with her husband and two little boys. There, Emma was introduced to spirituality and the coaching technique of 'The Law of Attraction,' which enhanced her creativity and inspired Emma to write her first fantasy fiction novel, 'The Crystal Masters: Part One,' available on Amazon.com.

She has mastered her craft over the years with the help of a writing coach and online tutorials from some of the world's leading authors. Emma also loves creating her artwork, believing it adds a more personal touch, and now has written this inspiring chapter for the bestselling book series 'Journey of Riches.' Emma is working on the sequels to 'The Crystal Masters' series and has ideas for other fantasy novels in the pipeline. She hopes her stories will bring escapism and pleasure to people's lives, just as it does for her.

Contact details:

Facebook – Emma Flowers

Nadia Elmagrabi

CHAPTER THREE

Nadia Elmagrabi, MA, is a psychotherapy-informed coach specializing in ancestral healing and Past Life Regression. She is gifted at supporting her clients to actualize their full potential and process undigested grief. She assists them in extracting the inner gold from their most challenging and complex experiences. She holds space and intuitively guides her clients as they traverse the depths of their psyches to find what keeps them immobilized in certain areas of their life.

She uses Past Life Therapy, Human Design, and Quantum Healing, as well as 20+ years of experience as a clinical psychotherapist, to expertly guide clients to find the inner gold from the night of their soul and bring it into the light so they can rejoice in the fullness of their Being.

Nadia works primarily with professional & entrepreneurial women who thrive in most areas but are challenged by something so deep they can't grasp it. Usually, it is around a struggle with a primary relationship. Nadia guides them to the source of their most pressing concern, where they can process and integrate the undigested grief associated with the difficulty or trauma in their unconscious mind.

Besides her extensive training and schooling, Nadia has overcome difficulties and challenges in her relationships that seemed insurmountable. She is dedicated to assisting others in overcoming their grief and stepping into their power in all areas of life so they can fully thrive and experience the boundless freedom that is their birthright.

Find Nadia:

Email: nadia@nadiaelmagrabi.com

Facebook: https://www.facebook.com/n.elmagrabi

Instagram: https://www.instagram.com/nadia_elmagrabi

Website: www.NadiaElmagrabi.com

Free Past Life Regression Recording: https://www.groupregressionsession.com/guided-past-life-regression-session

Renee Andreasen

CHAPTER FOUR

Renee is the owner and founder of Healthy Inspired You and a public speaker, transformational life coach, and gut health expert. She helps people overcome Anxiety through natural methods to get their life back.

She specializes in meditation and mindfulness to rebalance the mind, body, and spirit. Along with her 20 years in corporate coaching and leadership development, she is a Certified Autoimmune Paleo (AIP) Coach, Certified Health Coach (CHC), and educated in Functional Nutrition. She also creates custom health and transformational life programs for 1:1 and groups and Wellness Retreats in Hawaii.

After going through a lifetime challenge of her anxiety and resulting liberation, she figured out how to heal by unlocking the body's innate ability to heal itself given the right conditions. It's her mission to share natural healing techniques with the world so that people can realize their full human potential in this lifetime.

My social media things:

Website: https://healthyinspiredyou.com/

Facebook:
https://www.facebook.com/renee.andreasen or Renee Andreasen

YouTube:
https://www.youtube.com/channel/UCZJ2ovai-8DG_e5EuGFxkng

Instagram:
https://www.instagram.com/reneeandreasen/

Marie Chandler

CHAPTER FIVE

Marie Chandler is an internationally recognised Psychosomatic Therapist, professional speaker, author, and coach. An inspirational speaker, Marie has presented at many key events and conferences covering topics such as 'The Magic of Hands and Feet,' 'Face Shapes Revealed,' and 'How to Spot a Liar.'

Her media appearance as The face reading expert on The Bachelor AU led to additional interviews on Studio 10 and Cheap Seats in Australia and Loose Women in the UK.

Marie navigates her face-reading clients to rediscover their body-mind balance by highlighting rejected parts to release suppressed and unexpressed embodied emotions. As her clients learn or remember how to self-nurture, this opens the gate for them to move forward with aligning their purpose.

Marie has travelled extensively, visiting over 80 countries, and resides in Sydney, Australia.
Learn more by visiting www.facereadingsydney.com.au.

Sandra Elston

CHAPTER SIX

Sandra left a successful corporate career after thirty years and became a healer. Why?

This sounds like a massive change, but the truth is that the need to change her life crept up on her slowly. For a long time, she loved her work. Then it was OK. Then it really wasn't OK at all. Moreover, in the background, her life purpose had been calling to her softly at first and then louder and louder until Sandra reached the point where she woke up knowing that the job was wrong for her every day.

So in 2011, Sandra left the corporate world. First, she trained in Reiki. Then her journey led her to The Academy of Inner Resonance, where she took a two-year diploma in crystal healing, which was a richly rewarding experience. The Academy of Inner Resonance now has a school in the beautiful Highlands of Scotland. She is a specialist in aligning energy for conscious creation.

She lives in Dorset with her family and goes to the beach as often as possible. Life is good. She loves spending time investing because it's fun. Above all, she consistently aligns her energy with what she wants to create in the world.

Jenny Bot

CHAPTER SEVEN

Jenny struggled to find stability in her relationships but never lost her passion for living life.

She is especially interested in spiritual growth and wellness, studying with many healers. She is about personal growth and is a lifelong learner, graduating with her Bachelor's in Biology and most interested in global issues and the environment.

Her three small children are her greatest joy and inspiration to make the world a better place.

Jenny inspires others to never give up on their hopes and dreams. She now resides in California; you might find her doing yoga in her garden with her second husband and three children.

Her handle is Jenny Botlady on Twitch, collaborating with an international gaming community that always aspires to connect with new people.

Follow her story after the book on her socials here: https://linktr.ee/botlady

Please connect with the Author, Jenny Bot, on her social media.

Twitter @Botlady4

Instagram @bot.lady

Facebook @BOTLADYBB

TikTok @botlady_metaverse_girl

Maria Jesus Campos

CHAPTER EIGHT

Maria Jesus Campos is the Founder and CEO of Self·Health·Wealth.

From building her wealth and confronting life challenges, she lost her health completely at only 27. Becoming a mother saved her life. She focused completely on her Health to live for her kids.

This health warrior changed her destiny of a short life by beating an autoimmune disease that was impossible to do. After 11 Years of Investigating and experimenting on herself, she shares how to heal our selves.

She has changed her life completely to help others learn how to heal their bodies.

Because time is precious, she decided to share and teach them the fast track to Health.

Nutrition and Movement Medicine is her deep passion that greatly speeds up healing. Through her several programs, she builds the right to health worldwide. She believes that everyone should live in their best Health and nothing less.

She is a joyful and passionate woman that spreads love, smiles, and health. Everything she does comes from her heart and passion.

She is highly able to connect, teach and inspire others. As an international coach, she shines and radiates, giving life on the stage through her fantastic energy.

Since Maria Jesus discovered that being happy was a choice, she has an impressive courage to always say yes to up-level, and that is how she ended up being part of the project Think and Grow Rich by being part of the cast of the Mom's Rising movie and book.

Nerida Winters

CHAPTER NINE

Nerida Winters is an identical twin. Although born in Sydney, she grew up in regional New South Wales country towns and now resides in Bungendore, New South Wales, Australia.

She has always been passionate about helping people, dogs, and horses. While she has owned horses most of her life, her life changed significantly when she purchased a new horse in 2007. He challenged her skills, and Nerida had to step up and further develop her horsemanship to develop their relationship. This created a solid foundation in her ability to understand and train horses.

Following a life event in 2014, Nerida put two of her greatest passions together to help make a difference for others through the healing benefits of horses. In 2017, Nerida partnered with her daughter Ellen to start a heart-centred business, 'Lyndonlea Equine.' They provide coaching through gentle training methods with a focus on rider biomechanics.

Their therapy miniature horses support well-being in the community by visiting local nursing homes, hospitals, and schools. Through experiential learning with the horses and being in nature,

'Lyndonlea Equine' works to improve well-being and mental health, support those with a disability, and empower and grow their clients' life skills. They also assist learning opportunities through their Horse Powered Reading programs and, more recently, have included energy healing by the horses into their service.

Amanda Ray

CHAPTER TEN

Amanda Ray is a content and blogger writer after having a successful career as an Executive Assistant. Working as an Executive Assistant to the CEO and Mayor of an Aboriginal community on Indigenous land in Far North Queensland prompted her to change career paths.

Amanda states, “My time working and living in the Aboriginal community was the most life-changing and profound experience of my life.”

This period changed her perceptions of life, saying, “The living conditions were harsh, no modern conveniences or the luxuries of living in a city. This made me realise that, as a society, we put too much importance on money, appearances, and material wealth.

Listening to Dreamtime stories awakened my spiritual awareness and a need to seek a more meaningful life. I aim to share my learnings with the world to create social consciousness and collective self-awareness for society to be socially responsible.

It is a way for everyone to look at how their actions or lack of actions impact the social fabric of life.”

Social media

Twitter @AmandaRay02

Instagram @Amanda.Ray02

Email amanda.ray02@gmail.com

Yiuvany Aguilar

CHAPTER ELEVEN

Yiuvany Aguilar was born into a typical Peruvian family. She is the eldest of four children and the proud mother of three girls, two in heaven now. She proved to be intrepid, daring, persevering, and determined from an early age, which led her to fulfill her most cherished dreams. As a nurse by profession, the author has experienced true pain, frustration, and grief endured by patients and their families.

She decided to specialize as a holistic nurse, life coach, and Mindfulness and Self Compassion teacher in the United States. That was in search of a better approach and management of the difficult circumstances encountered through her work.

Utilizing the tools learned from her own experience and her training helped her deal with pain, not only physical but also that of the soul. Later, these tools would help her face the greatest life challenges, accepting the death of her beloved twins and a divorce after 18 years of marriage.

She started a new journey to heal her wounds, writing and sharing the lessons she learned along the way. She published her first book, "PEARLS OF THE SOUL," facing adversity with love, in 2022.

Annette Korolenko

CHAPTER TWELVE

Annette is an Author and Life Coach and poetically orchestrates the essence of thoughts into words describing every heartfelt feeling. Her book *Believe in Signs, Synchronicities and Miracles* is almost completed.

From working as an Interpreter for U.S Press abroad, searching for meaning, to her passion and love of storytelling /writing/ screenwriting, she hopes to inspire.

She is the creator of Love Notes / Love Cards.
She has published articles and poetry in five international magazines. Books in progress:

Believe in Signs, Synchronicities, and Miracles
Journey of Women
Gypsy Stories
Adventures of Zip-Zap and Zoom-Zoom (children's stories)

She is also an International Best-Selling Author for *Messages From the Heart* and *Live Your Passion* from the International best-selling *A Journey of Riches* book series.

To connect, email Annette at:
akblessed@yahoo.com. Tel. 224-500-8429

John Spender

CHAPTER THIRTEEN

John Spender is a 33-time International Best-Selling co-author who didn't learn how to read and write at a basic level until he was ten. He has since traveled the world and started many businesses leading him to create the best-selling book series A Journey Of Riches. He is an Award-Winning International Speaker and Movie Maker.

John worked as an international NLP trainer and has coached thousands of people from various backgrounds through various challenges. From the borderline homeless to very wealthy individuals, he has helped many people to get in touch with their truth to create a life on their terms.

John's search for answers to living a fulfilling life has taken him to work with Native American Indians in the Hills of San Diego, the forests of Madagascar, swimming with humpback whales in Tonga, exploring the Okavango Delta of Botswana and the Great Wall of China. He's traveled from Chile to Slovakia, Hungary to the Solomon Islands, the mountains of Italy, and the streets of Mexico.

Everywhere his journey has taken him, John has discovered a hunger among people to find a new way to live, with a yearning for freedom of expression. His belief that everyone has a book in them was born.

He is now a writing coach, having worked with over 300 authors from 40 countries for the A Journey of Riches series http://ajourneyofriches.com/ and his publishing house, Motion Media International, has published 28 non-fiction titles.

John also co-wrote and produced the documentary Adversity starring Jack Canfield, Rev. Micheal Bernard Beckwith, Dr. John Demartini, and many more. Moreover, you can bet there will be a best-selling book to follow!

AFTERWORD

I hope you enjoyed the shared heartfelt stories, wisdom, and vulnerability. Storytelling is the oldest form of communication, and I hope you feel inspired to take a step toward living a fulfilling life. Feel free to contact any of the authors in this book or the other books in this series.

The proceeds of this book will be used for social giving at Jewel Children's Home in Northeast Bali.

Other books in the series are...

Live Your Passion: A Journey of Riches, Book Thirty-two
https://www.amazon.com/Live-Your-Passion-Stories-Fulfilling-ebook/dp/B0C5QXMNRQ

Master Your Mindset: A Journ*ey of Riches*, Book Thirty-one
https://mybook.to/MasterYourMindset

Transform Your Wounds into Wisdom: A Journey of Riches, Book Thirty
https://www.amazon.com/dp/ B0BKTJ377N

Motivate Your Life: A Journey of Riches, Book Twenty-Nine
https://www.amazon.com/dp/B0BCXMF11P

Awaken to Your Inner Truth: A Journey of Riches, Book Twenty-Eight
https://www.amazon.com/dp/B09YLYMQ4H?geniuslink=true

Awaken to Your Inner Truth: A Journey of Riches, Book Twenty-Eight
https://www.amazon.com/dp/B09YLYMQ4H?geniuslink=true

The Power of Inspiration: A Journey of Riches, Book Twenty-Seven
http://mybook.to/ThePowerofInspiration

Messages from The Heart: A Journey of Riches, Book Twenty-Six
http://mybook.to/MessagesOfHeart

Abundant Living: A Journey of Riches, Book Twenty-Five
https://www.amazon.com/dp/B0963N6B2C

The Way of the Leader: A Journey of Riches, Book Twenty-Four
https://www.amazon.com/dp/1925919285

The Attitude of Gratitude: *A Journey of Riches,* Book Twenty-Three
https://www.amazon.com/dp/1925919269

Facing Your Fears: *A Journey of Riches,* Book Twenty-Two
https://www.amazon.com/dp/1925919218

Returning to Love: *A Journey of Riches,* Book Twenty-One
https://www.amazon.com/dp/B08C54M2RB

Develop Inner Strength: *A Journey of Riches,* Book Twenty
https://www.amazon.com/dp/1925919153

Building your Dreams: A Journey of Riches, Book Nineteen
https://www.amazon.com/dp/B081KZCN5R

Liberate your Struggles: A Journey of Riches, Book Eighteen
https://www.amazon.com/dp/1925919099

In Search of Happiness: A Journey of Riches, Book Seventeen
https://www.amazon.com/dp/B07R8HMP3K

Tapping into Courage: A Journey of Riches, Book Sixteen
https://www.amazon.com/dp/B07NDCY1KY

The Power Healing: A Journey of Riches, Book Fifteen
https://www.amazon.com/dp/B07LGRJQ2S

The Way of the Entrepreneur: A Journey Of Riches, Book Fourteen
https://www.amazon.com/dp/B07KNHYR8V

Discovering Love and Gratitude: A Journey Of Riches, Book Thirteen https://www.amazon.com/dp/B07H23Q6D1

Transformational Change: A Journey Of Riches, Book Twelve https://www.amazon.com/dp/B07FYHMQRS

Finding Inspiration: A Journey Of Riches, Book Eleven https://www.amazon.com/dp/B07F1LS1ZW

Building your Life from Rock Bottom: A Journey Of Riches, Book Ten https://www.amazon.com/dp/B07CZK155Z

Transformation Calling: A Journey Of Riches, Book Nine https://www.amazon.com/dp/B07BWQY9FB

Letting Go and Embracing the New: A Journey Of Riches, Book Eight https://www.amazon.com/dp/B079ZKT2C2

Making Empowering Choices: A Journey Of Riches, Book Seven https://www.amazon.com/Making-Empowering-Choices-Journey-Riches-ebook/dp/B078JXMK5V

The Benefit of Challenge: A Journey Of Riches, Book Six https://www.amazon.com/dp/B0778S2VBD

Personal Changes: A Journey Of Riches, Book Five https://www.amazon.com/dp/B075WCQM4N

Dealing with Changes in Life: A Journey Of Riches, Book Four https://www.amazon.com/dp/B0716RDKK7

Making Changes: A Journey Of Riches, Book Three https://www.amazon.com/dp/B01MYWNI5A

The Gift In Challenge: A Journey Of Riches, Book Two https://www.amazon.com/dp/B01GBEML4G

From Darkness into the Light: A Journey Of Riches, Book One
https://www.amazon.com/dp/B018QMPHJW

Thank you to all the authors who have shared aspects of their lives, hoping to inspire others to live a bigger version of themselves.

I want to share a beautiful quote from Jim Rohan, "You can't complain and feel grateful at the same time." At any given moment, we can either feel like a victim of life or be connected and grateful for it. I hope this book helps you feel grateful and inspires you to pursue your dreams.

For more information about contributing to the series, visit http://ajourneyofriches.com/. Furthermore, if you enjoyed reading this book, we would appreciate your review on Amazon to help get our message out to even more readers.

www.ingramcontent.com/pod-product-compliance
Lightning Source LLC
Chambersburg PA
CBHW051955090426
42741CB00008B/1405

* 9 7 8 1 9 2 5 9 1 9 6 5 3 *